GUIDE FOR BUSINESS START-UPS AND EXISTING BUSINESSES

DR. ROBERT GREGORY

Copyright © 2021 Dr. Robert Gregory
All rights reserved
First Edition

PAGE PUBLISHING, INC.
Conneaut Lake, PA

First originally published by Page Publishing 2021

ISBN 978-1-6624-2161-7 (pbk)
ISBN 978-1-6624-2163-1 (hc)
ISBN 978-1-6624-2162-4 (digital)

Printed in the United States of America

To Mom and Dad who raised me to pursue
and appreciate excellence.
To my family, children, and grandchildren for their
loving patience throughout my journey.
To my clients, mentees, friends, and associates
who often took advantage of my advice.
To the readers of this book who will realize
"increase" for the business they have chosen.
And above all, to the Lord GOD Almighty himself for
faith, strength, health, family, friends, and blessings.

Praise for *Guide for Business Startups & Existing Businesses*

"While all of us are leaders in growing organizations, we seem to know what makes us successful." Dr. Gregory does an exemplary job of pushing the reader to think-out-of-the-box to unlock the potential within.

If you are looking for a playbook to achieve business growth, customer loyalty and success, *The Guide for Business Start-Ups & Existing Businesses* hits the mark. I expect every reader will take away new ideas and strategies to put into practice and grow their respective businesses."

Raynard (Doc) Brooks
Commander
American Legion Post 263

"*Guide for Business Start-Ups & Existing Businesses* is a wise read for any business owner trying to chart successful and profitable growth. Dr. Gregory elegantly outlines a clear path that simplifies the complexities of driving a business toward actionable ideas that add immediate value in thinking, planning and acting strategically. Reading this book will surely lead to great results for any business owner."

Brian A. Hawkins, MHA
President & Chief Executive Officer
Family Health Centers of Baltimore

"Dr. Gregory's smart, sincere and thoughtful approach, models the strategies he advocates. To sit and speak with "Doc" is to get a healthy dose of knowledge, whether one wants to start a business or already has an existing business. Doc's" wisdom guided me and several other business owners that I know. *Guide for Business Start-Ups*

& Existing Businesses, illustrates a remarkable and simply way to arm the business owner with a strategic weapon aimed at managing the art of business success."

Flonnie Thompson
President & Chief Executive Officer
Flonnie T. Trucking, LLC

"If you ever find yourself in a low place in your business, this book will show the way up, the way out, and the way beyond. I'm convinced that reading *Guide for Business Start-Ups & Existing Businesses* will help you turn your problems into possibilities and your challenges into glorious opportunities. Doc cements his appeal to a wide range of businesses and business owners."

Dimostene Levissianos
President & Chief Executive Officer
Odyssey Group

Guide for Business Start-Ups & Existing Businesses presents refreshingly pragmatic advice and inspires the business owner to "take the blinders off" and look around the corner for growth opportunities in a new and powerful way. Through insightful examples and a well-structured process "Doc" presents the framework for business owners to leverage their way to success. A must-read!

Tony Randall
Retired Verizon Executive
Owner: Next Phaze Enterprises
TT Systems
Next Phaze Technologies
Next Phaze Café & Jazz Lounge

CONTENTS

Introduction 9

Chapter 1: In the Beginning 15
Chapter 2: Electing Your Business Structure 19
Chapter 3: The Business Plan 25
Chapter 4: Financing Your Business 30
Chapter 5: Running the Business Practice 33
Chapter 6: Who and When to Hire 37
Chapter 7: Marketing and Advertising 41
Chapter 8: Branding Your Business 52
Chapter 9: Growing Your Business 59
Chapter 10: Communication Skills 62
Chapter 11: Taxes and Write-Offs 67
Chapter 12: Self-Evaluation Tool 76
Chapter 13: Secrets of Success 79

Exhibit 1: A Guide to Advantages of LLCS 85
Exhibit 2: Business Start-Up Checklist 86
Exhibit 3: Business Plan Template 87
Exhibit 4: Dr. Gregory's Prescription for Getting Things Done ... 124
Exhibit 5: Blueprint to Grow Your Business 125
Exhibit 6: Self-Assessment for Business Owners 126
Exhibit 7: Business Owner Self-Assessment Test 128
Exhibit 8: Terms of Endearment 132

INTRODUCTION

Reflection

Ever since I was a little kid, I've been a fast-moving, hardworking, go-getting kind of person. I recall, at age nine, I started my lawn cutting/snow-shoveling business by knocking on doors, offering a free onetime service in exchange for the resident to call one neighbor to let them know that I did a good job. This yielded a lot of good repeat business for me. I guess my dad was right. He often told me, "You get what you give."

I worked at a clothing store in a mall part-time while attending high school. I designed an index card system to record certain information on customers. I greeted and served. I knew their favorite colors, shirt size, shoe size, birthday date, spouse's name, birthday, anniversary date, etc. Whenever we had a sale or they had a special occasion, I would call to ask them to come in to see me. Taking care of the customers yielded more commission dollars than my hourly wages. I guess my mom was also right. She often to told me, "It's nice to be nice."

This drive for success became my passion throughout my professional career. During an employment interview, I recall being asked, "What I would consider to be my weakness". Scratching my head for an acceptable answer, I slowly stated—lack of patience. Then I went on to say that I have little patience for mediocracy, for mediocre efforts yield mediocre results—I got the job!

I have enjoyed the pleasure of working in several industries throughout my career. I have held senior management and executive management positions. I have started, turned around, owned, and sold many businesses. In this book, I intend to share my experiences and skills as a framework to influence business success. This book flows with the power, experience, and knowledge of a *trusted business adviser* to educate the reader. Based on best practices and lessons learned, this book actualizes the key essentials needed for business success.

Every business owner needs certain tools in their toolbox to help deal with adversity, struggle, and challenges. These obstacles could and will affect growth and sustainability. This book represents the essential tools needed for business success. The reader will discover how to use these tools to manage to the full potential business success.

Reading this book is like attending a two-day retreat, seminar, or lecture series to help business owners start, manage, and successfully reap the financial rewards for business success. Accept that the author here, anticipates your questions and designs a blueprint for potential solutions for sustainable success. This book will inspire you to create your own success.

Who should read this book?

- Those who want to start a new business
- Those who want to grow an existing business
- Those who want to run, manage, and grow a successful business model
- Those who want to want to achieve wealth through succession, planning, or legacy

Why read this book?

- To learn, understand, and use the principles of business success
- To realize industry "best practices"
- To learn and understand the strategic essentials of business survival
- To embrace excellence and sustainability
- To help reduce your learning curve as you build your brand
- To embrace the numerous takeaways and make them your own

The Challenge

This book has been a labor of love. It has been challenging and difficult. I have had a few trials and tribulations. I wrote the book, rewrote, then rewrote it again. I even told my friends and clients about the book I was writing. Everyone I talked to wanted a copy. My publisher, family, and friends all pushed me to get this book to market. My clients needed this book to obtain the information, motivation, and inspiration necessary for their future success. Therefore, I persisted and refused to give up. I'm glad I had the challenges. I'm glad I had the struggle. It's made me the author I am now. The struggle was worth it!

In business, challenge and struggle are pre-conditions for growth. It's an unavoidable part of the entrepreneurial journey. Nothing ever comes easy when you are trying to build success. Difficulties and adversities will be your constant companions. Napoleon Hill said, "Strength and growth come only through continuous effort and struggle." Don't hate the journey you've chosen. Be encouraged by those who have already passed through the struggle. Once the struggle is embraced, miracles are possible. Reading this book will make miracles happen.

Small businesses are the growth engine of the nation's economy. Business owners struggle with many challenges in today's environment. Among such challenges are:

- the economy itself,
- government regulations,
- taxes,
- cash flow,
- lack of time,
- lack of talent,
- lack of treasure (money),
- competition,
- supply and demand, and
- balancing growth and quality.

Understanding the critical issues related to these challenges is extremely important as you navigate the course to business success. The underlying cause of a business's inability to achieve greatness is much like the story of the *Titanic*. It wasn't the height of the iceberg—challenge seen in front of the ship. They could have avoided that challenge. However, they were not able to see or predict the size or length of the iceberg that was already underneath the ship when they visualize what was seen above the water. Accordingly, like in medicine, a strong foundation while navigating with sights of "what's going on below the surface?" can contribute to a successful business journey.

Whether you are a small business owner, big business owner, or contemplating a business start-up, there are certain (below the surface) key strategies and skills that are essentially necessary to help navigate and build a strong foundation for success. As you can imagine, often times, repairs and maintenance (a tune-up) is needed over time for even the best built structures. In business, "You get what you inspect—often not what you expect."

The principles contained in this book is an excellent guide for building or reorganizing an existing business. This book will empower you to change the way you do business and guide your steps to increased profitability and sustainable growth. You will not only achieve more success quicker, but you will also sharpen your skills and unlock your "true" potential. "Commit yourself, and go all out."

CHAPTER 1

In the Beginning

Starting a business requires a great deal of effort. Maintaining an existing business can be demanding as well. However, it can be extremely rewarding, but first, it will be hard. The only way you will be able to push through and make your business successful through all the hard parts and long hours, is if you are passionate about what you are doing. Follow your dreams, and using your passion and knowledge are the best places to begin. These two ingredients speak volumes in regard to business growth, success, and sustainability.

In the beginning, you are going to have many questions: Why? What? When? Where? and How? You are going to question and investigate: tasks, activities, goals, objectives, missions, responsibilities, undertakings, burdens, targets, ideas, resources, and pretensions associated with your business choices. You will surely ask yourself:

- What's a good business to be in?
- How do I start my new business?
- Am I in the "right" business?
- What's my purpose for this business?
- How much money can I make?
- How do I get my customers?

- Profit or nonprofit?
- Partnership, corporation, or LLC?

Choosing the "right" business is the most important challenge you will face. It very well may be hit or miss as you study the markets, analyze the numbers, and respond to consumer needs, business needs, and the market-driven rule of supply and demand (what's out there that people or companies want, need, or will pay top dollar for). One of the best options is to consider ways to make or sell a product or service that you know about and love. Ask yourself, "What can you develop or create in order to influence a '"demand'" or satisfy a need in the marketplace?" In doing so, you will have to do your research, enhance your knowledge, and bring or develop the appropriate skill sets to the table before moving forward. In choosing the "right" business, follow your passion, be real, reckon with competitors, be aware of your risk profile, and respect the internet.

Making a lifestyle choice is absolutely a perquisite in starting and maintaining a successful business. Here are a few of the *don'ts:*

- Be in a hurry to select your business.
- Compete with your employer in a moonlight business.
- Quit your job before you have at least completed start-up plans and are making money.
- Risk a lot of family assets.
- Operate a business in a field you do not know.
- Select a business that is high-risk or a hurdle you can't clear.

There are a few things that you should consider when contemplating your idea for starting or reengineering your business. First, you should identify your biggest source of satisfaction. Then, to the contrary, identify your biggest frustration. Great business ideas or improvements come from these concepts. Think about the biggest challenges in your community, state, or in the world fifteen years from now and resolve to build your business around satisfying that need. Last, but not least, you can explore how existing businesses are profiting around you—unplug and do the same thing better or in a different way.

Always believe, nothing is a sure thing. As you consider your entrepreneurial options, someone will try to tell you that operating a particular business is "a sure thing"—don't listen. You are much better off making choices about your business based on your own knowledge and interests—not someone else's. You need to know everything there is to know about your business:

- What you are selling?
- Who you are selling to?
- Profit margins
- Competition
- Market demands
- Pricing
- Strengths
- Weaknesses
- Opportunities
- Threats

Understanding these elements alone speaks volumes about your probability for success and will potentially build your reputation and brand.

Following your résumé is yet another way to give you an advantage for business success. What are you good at? If you already have years of experience in a particular field, you can make good use of your skills, training, network contacts, centers of influence, and your industry knowledge to fuel your business and ignite action and drive. If your interest to start a business is influenced by your particular skills and experiences, talk to people you know that have made the plunge in to the business ownership pool. Ask them about the pros and cons and what it took to dive off that high diving board and return to the surface. Are they swimming, just floating, or often sinking? I'm sure they will have a few lessons learned stories to share.

In the event you have several interests and are unable to focus on what would make the best business opportunity in the short term, you should consider your strongest skills and your educational background to help you determine which interest(s) you are best suited to pursue. It is also extremely important to research the marketplace to determine which type of businesses are presently needed in your area. If you don't know much about the business you want to start, but are set on it, be prepared to spend time learning about it before you begin so as to avoid making a costly critical mistake.

Starting a business is awesome and traumatic all at the same time. There will be good times alongside many hard times. However, the buck will stop with you, and you alone will be responsible and accountable for all decisions made—good or bad. I encourage you to think, anticipate, prepare, and get ready. At the end of the day—as the business owner—you must breathe, live, love, and let passion drive you to smart decisions.

CHAPTER 2

Electing Your Business Structure

So you now have your business idea. You need to know how to structure it. But before you do that, let's talk about how to evaluate whether you and your chosen business are a "good fit."

1. *Try this out.*
   You need to get some experience in the industry or in the profession that interest you—even if you have to work and learn for free. Learn everything you can about every aspect of the business. If you happen to be already in business or have "expert" experience, you are probably okay. In the event you are reengineering an existing business, then you may want to pick the brains of a few of your competitors.

2. *Talk to entrepreneurs in the same field.*
   Existing business owners and new business owners really need to talk to others (competitors) who provide same or similar services or products. Most of these business owners are often quite willing to share their knowledge once they are comfortable that you are not trying to steal away their secrets of success or their customers. Perhaps you can open

these doors by seeking mentorship, attempting to negotiate a partnership, or just talk to business owners in other states or cities.

3. *Evaluate whether you enjoy the hard work and can excel at it.*
It's unlikely you will like something you are not good at—so choose another business if you don't honestly enjoy the work. Until you figure it all out, your business has to keep you up at night "thinking about it," and it is on your mind and in your radar every morning and throughout your day.

4. *Judge your ability and desire to handle every aspect of your business.*
You should think twice about starting this type of business if you cannot or are not willing and able to work and understand the work as good or better than those you plan to hire. Many business owners often hire out the work they can't or do not want to do. But it's your business, and you need to know enough to determine when to hire and fire.

5. *Determine whether your business has a solid chance of turning the profit you want.*
Analyze your market. Understand economics 101—supply and demand. Know your competition, learn to rely on the numbers, conduct monthly break-even analysis, and determine when and if the revenues will cover your expenses. Save, save, save. Remember to have a "rainy day fund," which will serve as a reserve for contingencies.

In regard to your legal business entity structure, the type of business you choose will primarily depend on these three factors: liability, taxation, and record-keeping. Legalizing the business structure helps prevent misunderstandings among the participants by defining their ownership, roles, and duties in the business. By carefully considering the legal business entity structures available, then you can intelligently choose the one most appropriate for you.

The most common forms of businesses are:

- Sole proprietorships,
- Partnerships,
- Corporations (C corporations),
- Limited liability companies (LLC), and
- Subchapter S corporations (S corporations).

A sole proprietorship is a one-owner unincorporated business where the owner pays personal income tax on profits earned from the business. It is the easiest type of business to establish or take apart due to of lack of government regulation. This type of business is very popular among sole owners of businesses, individual self-contractors, and consultants. Many sole proprietors do business under their own names because creating a separate business or trade name isn't necessary.

Let's start with the difference between an LLC vs. Corporation. Corporations and LLCs are different in how they are taxed. Because corporations are separate entities, they are taxed at the corporate rate, while LLCs are taxed based on Adjusted Gross Income of the owners. The advantage of an LLC is generally considered to have over a corporation include the following:

1. LLCs can be governed more informally than corporations.
2. LLC's are better for more flexibility in how you manage and run your business.

3. An LLC can be a pass-through tax entity without the restrictions imposed on corporations.
4. LLC's have one or more individual members.

Do I need an LLC to start a business?

The simple answer is, no. You don't need an LLC to start your own business, although you may decide you want one. An LLC, or limited liability company, provides personal liability protection and a formal business structure, but you can also get those things by forming a corporation or other type of business entity.

What does an LLC protect you from?

"LLC Asset Protection: How to Protect your Personal Assets as an LLC Owner." Forming a limited liability company is an important first step to protect your personal assets from being used to pay business creditors. But an LLC's liability protection is not absolute.

Can my LLC become a nonprofit?

Nonprofit organizations are usually formed as corporations, but can an LLC be a nonprofit? LLCs aren't usually formed as nonprofit (or, technically, tax-exempt) organizations because most people find the process complex and realize forming as a nonprofit corporation is more straightforward.

Can a 501(C) (3) be an LLC?

According to IRS regulations, an LLC cannot be granted tax-exempt status directly. In order to obtain tax exemption, its members can establish a nonprofit corporation and run an LLC under the full ownership of the corporation.

Who should use which entity?

C Corporations

C Corporations are great for businesses that sell products/services and have employees. Businesses that offer services may find the taxes of a C Corp to be too high because of specific tax laws applied to Personal Service Corporations (PSC). It's also advised not to hold appreciating assets in a C Corp because of the tax treatment of asset sales.

C Corporations generally have more formal record-keeping and reporting requirements. They have shareholders and investors tend to prefer C Corporations.

S Corporations

S Corporations are a good choice for people who would like the protection and structure of a corporation, but would be classified as a PSC by the IRS. They are also great for businesses that have significant start-up costs because of their flow-through taxation.

LLCS

LLCs are great for people who want an entity to hold real estate or other appreciating assets. They are a popular choice for investors and entrepreneurs because of the flexible taxation and great asset protection. Please refer to the chart below for a summary guide.

ADVANTAGE	C CORP	S CORP	LLC	PARTNERSHIP	SOLE PROPRIETOR
Owners have limited liability for business debts and obligations	✓	✓	✓		
Created by a state-level registration that usually protects the company name	✓	✓	✓		
Business duration can be perpetual	✓	✓	✓		
May have an unlimited number of owners	✓		✓	✓	✓
Owners need not be U.S. citizens or residents	✓		✓		
May issue shares of stock to attract investors	✓	✓			
Owners can report business profits and loss on their personal return		✓	✓	✓	✓
Owners can split profit and loss with the business for a lower overall tax rate	✓				
Permitted to distribute special allocations, under certain guidelines			✓	✓	
Not required to hold annual meetings or record meeting minutes			✓	✓	✓

CHAPTER 3

The Business Plan

A business plan, as defined by an *Entrepreneur* is a "written document describing the nature of the business, the sales and marketing strategy, and the financial background containing the projected profit and loss statement." However, your business plan can serve several different purposes. Your business plan should be a formally written document containing your business goals. It should also include the methods on how these goals can be attained and the time frame in which these goals need to be achieved.

The Three Rules for Writing a Business Plan

1. Keep it short. Business plans should be short and concise.
2. Know you audience. Write your plan using language that your audience will understand.
3. Don't be intimidated.

Writing a business plan isn't for everyone. Often times the thought of not writing a business might convince you that you don't need one. The value proposition is that a business plan is a given for a successful start-up because it offers a designed template that appeals to the vision, mission, goals, and values of the business.

When you're starting a new business, do you really need a business plan to do it? Let's face it. When you're excited about your great new business idea and can't wait to get going, the last thing you want to do is sit down and spend weeks or months crafting a business plan. As the world of business has gotten less formal and the pace at which start-ups come to the market has sped up, many entrepreneurs have begun to question whether a business plan is no longer necessary anymore or outmoded as the typewriter. You may also think that as long as you're not looking for a bank loan, line of credit, or any type of outside financing, you don't need a business plan. It's true that lenders and investors will want to see a business plan—and if you're not looking for money from outside sources, you won't need to show a business plan to anyone.

However, the reasons to write a business plan really have nothing to do with other people. Instead, it's all about you. You may think you're making it easier on yourself and saving time by skipping the business plan. In reality, doing a little homework now and crafting a business plan will make your life much easier and save you tons of time later on. Here are five good reason why start-ups and existing business owners need a business plan:

1. Helps you to focus on all aspects of your business (marketing, managing, financing, and more)
2. Enables you to uncover problems ahead of time (identifies possible obstacles so that you can plan to avoid them)
3. Builds competence, character, and confidence (prepares you to be ready for anything)
4. Helps you be better able to explain your business and manage your success
5. Essentially vital to provide direction

Actually, getting started to write your business plan can be intimidating and difficult. So here's a seven-step process to writing a perfect plan:

1. Research, research, research.
   a. Consider spending twice as much time researching, analyzing, and evaluating your product, market, goals and objectives as you spend actually writing the business plan.

2. Determine the purpose of your plan.
   a. Your business plan can be written to serve several different purposes. It may be written to attract investors, partners, or used as a road map to provide direction so your business can plan its future and avoid bumps in the road.

3. Create a company profile.
   a. Your company profile includes the history of your organization, what products or services you offer, your target market, audience, resources, how you're going to solve a problem, and what makes your business unique.

4. Document all aspects of your business.
   a. Document everything: expenses, cash flow, industry projections, location strategy, licensing agreements, etc.

5. Have a strategic marketing plan in place.
   a. Your strategic and aggressive marketing plan should include marketing objectives supported by several goals and tactics for achieving those goals.

6. Make it adaptable based on your audience.
    a. Make sure that your plan can be modified depending on the audience reading your plan. The potential readers of a business plan may range from bankers and venture capitalists to employees and potential partners. Each reader has certain typical interests. You should know these interests up-front and be sure to take them into account when preparing a plan for that particular audience.

7. Explain why you care.
    a. Your plan needs to show that you're passionate, dedicated, and actually care about your business and the plan. You should discuss the mistakes that you've learned, the problems that you're hoping to solve, listing your values, and what makes you stand out from the competition.

No matter what kind or size of a business you are starting or reengineering, it's important to create a written plan to do so—your business plan. Creating a business plan forces you to confront the reality of what you are planning to do. It's your responsibility to know everything you can about your business and the industry. You must read everything you can about your industry and talk to your audience.

As you prepare to start your new business or reengineer your existing business, you will need to consult with professionals. This may include a business counselor, an accountant, and a lawyer. Be sure to include them in the preparation and review of your business plan.

Frequent and ongoing business plan reviews are essential to the success of your business. Knowing that "the only thing constant in life is change," the elements of your business plan should be revisited in an effort to keep up and keep on tract. As the business owner, you are the lead strategist, and therefore, the future of your business evolves around you. Review your business plan, and make the appropriate amendments to help keep you on track. (*See* Exhibit 3—located at the end of this book: "A Business Plan Template.")

CHAPTER 4

Financing Your Business

For instance, if you are an experienced executive chef and have managed a restaurant for years, starting your own restaurant will be easier for you. You will know suppliers and vendors. You will know how to build menus and order food. You will also know what people like and don't like when it comes to food. And when you go to the bank, and the loan officer sees your résumé, he/she will know you have the experience to back up what is traditionally a very risky business.

Finding financing in any economic climate can be laborious, whether you're looking for start-up funds, capital to expand, or money to hold on through the tough times. There are two main classes of financing available for businesses: debt and equity. Debt is a loan that must be paid back, usually with interest, but it is typically cheaper than raising capital because of the tax deduction consideration. Equity, on the other hand, is the process of raising capital through the sale of a percentage in your business. You sell a percent of ownership in your business in return for cash (like stock financing).

GUIDE FOR BUSINESS START-UPS AND EXISTING BUSINESSES

Within the two classes of financing stated above, there exist several subsets or types of financing that you should explore for your business and decide which type is most appropriate for your needs:

- Family and friends
- Traditional bank loan
- Microloan
- SBA loan
- Business line of credit
- Business credit card
- Equipment financing
- Invoice financing
- Factoring
- Accounts receivable financing
- Royalty financing
- Commercial real estate loan
- Home equity loan
- Auto loan
- Government grant
- Angel investor
- Venture capitalist
- Public stock offering
- Private stock offering

Navigating through the various types of financing can be confusing. Whichever choice you make, consider building strong business credit and make sure your personal credit is in shape. This will enable you to access the right amount of capital at the best rates.

Prior proper planning is the preparation necessary for you to qualify for the "right" financing. First, you should decide why you need the money and ask yourself how this loan will help your business. Second, after determining the "right" type of financing, you need to find the best lender for you. Your lender should complement your business and personal style. For instance, a lender who takes personal responsibility for the lending relationship provides timely communication and delivers great customer service is desired by most. Now all you have to do is see what it takes to qualify and begin to get your documents ready and apply.

Qualifying for business financing is easier when you're prepared. Here are a few steps to help you be prepared to qualify:

1. Build credit scores.
2. Know the lender's qualifications and requirements.
3. Gather financial and legal documents.
4. Develop a strong business plan.

You also may be asked to provide proof of collateral, bank statements, personal and business tax returns, accounts receivable aging, accounts payable aging, as well as to sign a personal guarantee or obtain a cosigner.

CHAPTER 5

Running the Business Practice

Running a small business is not for the faint of heart. Between filing taxes, hiring employees, managing client relations, and production, it's enough to drive the sanest person a little crazy. Many business owners have learned key business lessons from Warren Buffett's annual letters to Berkshire Hathaway shareholders:

1. Keep calm in the face of volatility.
2. Keep good company.
3. Keep your focus.
4. Keep costs low.
5. Keep employee incentives simple.
6. Keep your reputation.
7. Get it in writing.
8. Hire the right people.
9. Protect yourself—at all times.
10. Keep your edge.
11. Pay your bills on time.
12. Pay your taxes on time.
13. Put your customers' needs first.
14. Boost your website's visibility.
15. Build your brand on social media.

"The Ten Most Important Letters" to influence business success are WITFM (what's in it for me) and WITFT (what's in it for them). These letters represent the value proposition component, the thing that makes them realize that what you're offering is worth their money or their time. Accordingly, your business should be run pitching each and every prospect on the benefits rather than the features of what you're selling. You must literally tell them what's in it for them. Prospects don't often care that you need to close at least three more sales this month or that you're shooting for a big win before you leave on vacation. Anyway, why should they? Neither of those things benefit them. That's a "transactional opportunity." Your prospects want to hear about what they stand to gain by buying your product or service. That's why benefits out sell features so dramatically. WITFT implies that you have taken the time to understand the needs and interest of your prospect—then match the benefits to their needs.

The following characteristics can be your guide to running a successful business practice:

1. *Be consistent.*
   Consistency is a key component to making money in business. This will create long-term positive habits that will help you "in the money" for the long run.

2. *Provide excellent customer service.*
   Be friendly, say thank you, listen, train your staff, show respect, be responsive, ask for feedback, and your customers will be more inclined to come to you instead of going to your competition…just for the service.

3. *Prepare to make sacrifices.*
   Business impose some risks and risks mean sacrificing. You must sacrifice to grow your business. The rigors of entrepreneurship demand sacrifices like security, stabil-

ity, work-life balance, income, sleep, family, and comfort. "Entrepreneurship is living a few years of your life like most people won't so you can spend the rest of your life like most people can't."

4. *Stay focused.*
"Rome was not built in a day." It takes time to let people know who you are. Staying focus while building and running your business is an ongoing challenge for every business owner. You have to stay focused on you, while maintaining focus on your business all at the same time. For example, chose your leisure activities wisely, be productive with your time, get up early, and I recommend you read *Rhinoceros Success* by Scott Alexander for encouragement.

5. *Be creative.*
Always look for ways to improve your business—new ideas and new approaches. Gather new ideas and resources, meditate, clarify your vales, brainstorm, and shift negative thoughts into a positive mindset.

6. *Analyze your competition.*
Competition breeds the best results. Study your competition. They may be doing something right that you can implement in your own business to make money. "The purpose of the competitive analysis is to determine the strengths and weaknesses of the competitors within your market, strategies that will provide you with a distinct advantage, the barriers that can be developed in order to prevent competition from entering your market, and any weaknesses that can be exploited."

7. *Keep detailed records.*
   Keeping detailed and accurate records allow you to pay attention to the health, welfare, and performance of your business so that you can preserve sustainability and make any improvements essentially necessary.

8. *Get organized.*
   This is essential to the survival of your business. Good organizational skills can save a business owner time and reduce stress. Being organized will help you balance many tasks efficiently and effectively.

Business owners are often seen as "part of the solution or part of the problem." Remember, it's your company and the burdens, successes, and all the related decisions fall "on your watch." Your customers, competitors, and the business world will attribute your success or failure to your actions—not someone else's. "What keeps brilliant people from being extraordinary are their beliefs about other people's judgment and opinions." You need to be "the Captain of your own ship and the master of your fate." Don't let anyone else take that wheel. As you navigate the waters, take responsibility and avoid the judgments and opinion of others. You're in charge. Stay your course and learn to anticipate the obstacles you need to avoid. (*See* Exhibit 4—located at the end of this book: "Twenty-One Steps to Getting Things Done.")

CHAPTER 6

Who and When to Hire

Almost all small businesses start out as one-man bands. You are usually wearing multiple hats, handling marketing, sales, operations, finances, and perhaps even rolling up your sleeves to do the daily work. The business owner actually becomes the "jack-of-all-trades." At some point you will be stretching yourself too thin, and your business will be suffering for it. Then you will have to assess what to outsource and what to hire for. It helps to have professional partners, coaches, advisers, and resources of the like to help you navigate and make appropriate decisions outside of your expertise. Considering you have the expertise and you know when or who to hire, just make sure that the cost of the new hire is supported by the potential revenues that their worth brings to the table.

Every business owner wants more customers, more qualified prospects, and more revenue. But starting a business isn't one of those "if you build it, they will come" situations. As the business grows, business owners come to recognize that as much as they would like to, they can't always do all the work all by themselves. Every entrepreneur will reach a point where a business is ready to scale and grow as quickly as it can. By putting the right people on the bus, you'll be able to scale quickly without losing your ability to provide great products, services, and excellent customer service.

Your business plan and your budget represent the key tools to help you determine when and who to hire. The process of hiring can be a challenging event on its own. Hiring help too early or inappropriately can be a paralyzing event that could put your business at risk. You must think about cash flow, employee benefits, 1099s vs. W2s, workmen's compensation insurance, and a host of other related costs associated with hiring. Here are a few signs that will help you identify when you need to hire:

- Your customers can't reach you.
- For tasks that generate revenue that supports more than their compensation.
- You are turning down work.
- You are using valuable time on nonessential task.
- For tasks that decrease liability.
- The quality of your products and services are suffering.
- Cannot timely meet delivery or shipping request.
- Your customers are complaining.
- You don't have the time to do the daily financial, bookkeeping, or operations paperwork.
- You need someone with a specific skill set.
- There's enough work to keep a new hire busy.

Point is, there are many reasons when to consider onboarding a new hire in your business. Many small business owners create an advisory board of known professionals in their circle of influence to help them scale the hiring hurdle and advise them on other business decisions. These advisers could be friends, family, mentors, retired professionals, or owners of other businesses. Advisory board members usually serve on a volunteer basis and sometimes may be compensated for attending monthly board meetings. The experience and expertise of these advisers can prove to be critical to the success of your business. These advisers may include, but not limited to, the following professionals:

- Financial consultant/adviser
- Attorney
- Experienced tax professional
- Retired business owners
- IT professional
- Marketing/advertising guru
- Photographer
- Industry-related vendor/supplier

The resources that these advisory board members can bring to the table will prove to be most valuable to help strike a balance while also helping you make a good hiring decision.

Some business owners look to scale their company for growth by identifying the needed skill sets and matching them up with job titles.

	POSITION	TASK/RESPONSIBILITY
1	**Project Manager**	Business development In charge of timelines Helps to grow the business sales pipeline
2	**Lead Strategist**	Marketing and Advertising
3	**Social Media Manager**	In charge of social media content and outreach
4	**Web Master**	Website E-Commerce development Provides ongoing website customization Updates and maintains company website E-mail marketing

Employees may be full-time, part-time, or contractual. You may also consider outsourcing certain tasks until such time that the business can afford otherwise. Every new hire should be able to make a significant impact toward the goals of the business. Keep in mind the associated costs of hiring a new employee:

- The cost of recruiting
- The cost of training
- The cost of salary + benefits
- The cost of workplace integration
- The break-even point

As part of the new hire induction process, they should be informed and become committed to the mission, vision, values, and goals of your business as well as the policies and procedures that govern them.

Professional Assistance

Many business owners take accounting, marketing, and other business-related courses to help develop their competency. This is a good idea, however, unless you hold an advance degree in these areas of need, you may still find that your level of expertise still lacking. Utilizing the assistance of certain professionals may prove to serve you well. You actually don't have to be an expert in all areas to run a successful business entity. Consult or hire the people to do the jobs that you either are not good at or do not have the time, want, or need to do. Stay in your lane! The professionals you consult don't and should not manage the day-to-day activities of your business. But they should be able to advise and counsel accordingly.

CHAPTER 7

Marketing and Advertising

Marketing and advertising are perplexed areas to begin with—ask twenty experts the difference between the two, and you'll get twenty different responses. An appreciable number of persons in the business world, put marketing and advertising in the same pot as a method to get services or products to prospective and clients. It is important for the business owner to understand that these terms are not synonymous.

Marketing is known as a "pull" promotional strategy. Businesses use this strategy to increase demand for its products or services by drawing or pulling consumers to them to want a particular product or service. The goal here is to increase consumer demand by getting consumers to actively seek your product or service. A few of the methods available include:

- social media networks,
- word of mouth,
- media coverage,
- sales promotions,
- discount offers, and
- e-mail marketing.

Accordingly, "pull" marketing strategy is an avenue that draws a prospect to action. The receiver proactively retrieves it and responds. Advertising, on the other hand, is known as a "push" promotional strategy. Businesses use this concept to present promotional material to large groups of people through various channels including:

- flyers,
- magazines,
- television,
- radio,
- billboards,
- banner ads,
- door-to-door,
- face-to-face,
- public relations, and
- trade shows.

Accordingly, the "push" advertising strategy uses channels to launch products or services through to the sales process.

The primary difference between "push" and "pull" strategies lies in how consumers are approached. You may want to use the "push" strategy or the "pull" strategy. Initially, "push" communications help to create demand and "pull" communications offers a way for consumers to satisfy that need. Smart business owners use a combination of both. You will have to decide how much of your financial resources and time to allocate to which one or both types of strategies. The key is to be able to promote your product or service in a fashion that establishes a loyal following and repeat business.

Whether you are marketing or advertising, here are a few straightforward ways to improve success in your business:

1. Network.

2. Leverage your community.
3. Create buzz.
4. Ask for referrals.
5. Build relationships.
6. Build a great lead magnet.
7. Leverage influences.
8. Monitor trends.
9. Sharpen your selling skills.
10. Know your limits.
11. Realize that online marketing is the future for business.
12. Offer testimonials on your website.
13. Understand search engine optimization.
14. Use Facebook, LinkedIn, and Instagram ads to retarget.
15. Start blogging now.

Marketing and advertising will most certainly amplify your business. Understanding your market and customer needs speak volumes for business success. Using customer experiences and feedback to fuel your business growth is phenomenal. I have a challenge for you:

Decide on three simple things you can do right now, which cost particularly nothing, that you could do to get existing customers talking about you. Let me give you a hint and you fill in the blanks:

1. Use a welcome e-mail.
2. Use a "thank you for your business" e-mail.
3. Create a customer experience satisfaction (exit) survey.
4. Ask for referrals at every customer interchange.
5. _____
6. _____
7. _____

Building a strategic marketing plan is an essentially important as you build and grow your business. As part of your business plan, your marketing strategy is key. These six actionable steps will help you succeed in building your strategic marketing plan:

1. Business Objectives
    a. Business objectives are the quantifiable targets that the company wants to achieve in the coming year. For example, to double revenue by next fiscal year or achieve a fifteen percent revenue or profit growth.
    b. These objectives relate to the company as a whole and should be aligned to the business objectives in order to create an acceptable impact.

2. Marketing Priorities
    a. Marketing has to decide where and how it can make an impact by identifying which efforts to prioritize and which it cannot support.

3. Marketing Goals
    a. These goals define what marketing will do to support the business objectives. The goal metrics should integrate with the business targets.
    b. The four categories of business targets are impact, output, activity, and readiness.
    c. Impact is the effect on the business goals; output is the result of actions; activity is the number of actions taken; and readiness is how prepared the team is to perform.

4. Marketing Strategy
    a. This is the approach and continued efforts the marketing team will have to take to achieve its goals.

b. The strategy revolves around how the team plans to hit its goals.
   c. Action without strategy breeds failure.

5. Key Actions
   a. Refers to the specific efforts marketers will have to take to execute on strategy.
   b. Must include details on how each execution will impact the greater business objectives.
   c. Must be able to decide which actions to stop doing, which actions to expand on, and which new actions should be added to the plan.

6. Dependencies and Risks
   a. Identifying potential risk will help to better plan and adapt to changes or drawbacks that could occur throughout the year.

Marketing planning can be puzzling, but adapting all marketing efforts to business objectives helps you to optimize for the same metrics and goals.

Acquiring new customers, utilizing your marketing and advertising campaigns, can be incredibly challenging. You can spend countless hours and talent on perfecting your product or service, but your future depends on your ability to attract and retain new customers for the long term. You should be aware of your "customer acquisition cost" (CAC). This is the total sales and marketing cost required to earn a new customer over a designated period. This is important because it assigns real value to your marketing efforts and allows you to measure your "return on investment" (ROI). The formula looks like this.

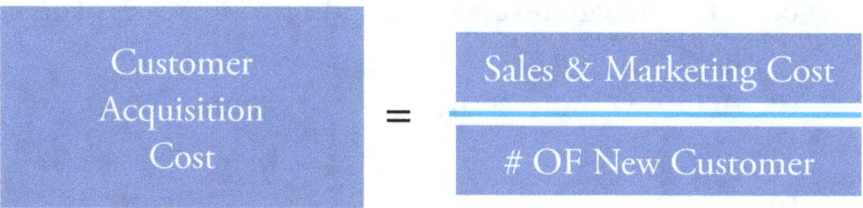

For example, if a company spent $300K on sales and marketing and generated three hundred new customers in one quarter, their customer acquisition cost would be $1K.

Content marketing is the cornerstone of advertising, because once you've published content; email, social media, etc. can promote it. Such content includes blog posts, e-books, guides, videos, etc. Content marketing is estimated to generate about "three times as many leads as other marketing methods and cost approximately sixty-two percent less."

Some companies use "highly targeted advertising" if they are not generating the number of new customers they want. This allows them to redefine their target audience and drill down to the finest details:

- Where do they live?
- How old are they?
- What do they do for a living?
- What is the composition and structure of their family?
- What do they like or dislike?
- What is their household income?
- What problems do they have, and how can your product or service help?

Retargeting your existing customer base is a great place to start. This sounds like customer retention, not acquisition; however that's not necessarily the case. Getting in old customer back to your business is like reacquiring them as a brand-new customer. All you have to do is use any old information you may have of them (e-mail, phone number, address, etc.), and reach out with an enticing offer to earn their business again.

Learning how to scale your business is important to future success. Some business owners want every customer in the universe. Everyone becomes a prospect. While other business owners segment their prospects based on certain demographic data. For instance, age, income, education, gender, or geographic location. Identifying the type of customer you want—the "ideal" customer—helps you to focus on your target market. You can build your product/service and brand around them and deliver solutions in respect to their needs. In other words, as opposed to offering your products/services to the general public or mass market, you can choose a "vertical" market and promote products and services specific to an industry, trade, profession, or other group of customers with specialized needs. An example could be a software that manages services in hotels or sanitizing and disinfecting services for funeral homes.

Strategic business partnerships are a great way to grow your business. This may allow your business to grow your customer base and improve your profits. Some other advantages of a well-structured strategic business partnership are new products or services, new markets, increased loyalty; and you may be able to block the competition. Please note that everyone in your industry is not a competitor. Chances are, there are many complementary businesses in your niche with similar customer bases.

Your website might look professional and offer a volume of useful information for visitors, but does it generate new leads and help to acquire new customers? Creating a "lead generating site" is essential to your business success. Having a dedicated "post-click landing page" to capture information will certainly enable you to fill the top of your sales funnel. Your "post-click landing page" is usually the first and last thing people see as they connect to your business. You have less than five seconds to grasp their attention when they come to your site. The attention-grabbing headline of your "post-click landing page" should stand out.

Your social media presence is important to your success especially in this day and age. If you're not presently on social media, you're missing out on a huge market that your competitors are likely already capitalizing on. A social media presence is not very expensive. Establishing a business account on LinkedIn, Facebook, Instagram, and Twitter is free. Joining discussions and groups that pertain to your industry will give your business attention. Providing helpful answers to questions and giving insights on various posts will help make you and your business known.

Running promotions and offering deals encourage repeat business. It also entices reluctant consumers to do business with you. People love discounts because they save money and feel like they're getting access to something exclusive and limited. Some ideas for offering deals and promotions include:

- using your social media accounts to run ad coupon ads,
- join in on popular hashtags like #Throwback Thursdays, and
- creating an e-mail drip campaign that rewards subscribers for access to their inboxes with an exclusive offer.

The most successful promotional campaigns also inspire sharing. When people share offers with their family and friends, they're more likely to be interested since it's coming from someone they know and trust rather than an ad from an unfamiliar brand. It makes them more likely to redeem the offer and continue sharing with others too.

If people are "on the fence" in regard to making a decision to purchase, perhaps you can give them something for free. This doesn't mean give away hundreds or thousands of products. Research consumers' needs that you can satisfy as it relates to or complement your product or service.

Example

T&T Disinfecting and Cleaning Services received a call-to-service from a local funeral home chain that required immediate service for disinfecting and sanitizing during the coronavirus pandemic. The owner of the business made an appointment to schedule the disinfecting and sanitizing application. Inquiring about other funeral home needs during this virus crisis, the business owner found out that the customer has been having no success in locating a thermometer to use to test employees and visitors of the funeral home. Long story short, the business owner was able to secure a large quantity of infrared forehead thermometers guns from a commercial distributor and agreed to give one to his new funeral home customer in exchange for them sharing their experience with other businesses or funeral homes in the area.

Showcasing testimonials is the best way to acquire new customers while building your reputation. When you have proof that customers have a particular positive experience, ask them to provide a testimonial in return. These testimonials can be posted on your company website (homepage—front or center, sidebars, or above your headline) on social media sites, and on other media advertising. Whether the testimonial is a short quote, review, case study, interview, etc. it's proof that you deliver on your promises and help prospects feel more confident they can trust you.

In business, the best way to stay ahead of the game is to keep track of the competition. You must actively monitor your competitor's marketing tactics, backlinks and traffic, Web design, social mentions, products or services, etc. Doing this can be especially useful in acquiring new prospects because it puts you in prime position to swoop in and capitalize on any opportunities. For instance, if you know that a competitor has introduced an unpopular initiative, like a price increase, it may be the perfect time to step in and see if any of their clients are willing to jump ship.

Some customers like to actually experience brands, not just read about them online or get spammed by their ads. So much that the majority of companies primarily compete on the basis of customer experience. Hosting an event is a great way to do this as it gives potential customers the opportunity to meet your brand on a more personal level. Depending on your product or services, you can either host an in-person event where customers can meet you or host an online webinar where it stills feels personalized—like you're right in front of your audience.

Using existing customers to attract new customers is by far the best way to elevate business success. Referrals are a great way get more customers, but consistently generating referrals can be tough. With referrals, it's easier to set appointments and have productive discussions because a higher level of trust and credibility is already established. A successful wealth manager used a unique concept to attract new business to his financial planning practice. All of his post meeting handwritten thank-you cards said:

> Thanks-A-Million for your business, I will always be hear to serve you. However, business is a contact sport and most of my clients discover me by word-of-mouth. I sincerely appreciate your warm referrals so that I can continue to provide you exceptional service.

The adviser grew his client base on referrals. Often times he offered a twenty-five-dollar reward for every referral his clients brought in. You can't expect valuable customer referrals without giving back something valuable in return. The incentive can be a physical gift, a monetary reward, or a credit/discount on future purchases; just make sure it's valuable to them.

Your ultimate goal is customer acquisition. Don't miss out on customers. Customers allow your business to make money, meet costs, pay employees, and reinvest in growth. Every company needs to acquire new customers to keep their business running smoothly. Start acquiring more new customers today by:

- building an acquisition strategy,
- learning to reduce the costs of customer acquisition, and
- understanding the ROI.

CHAPTER 8

Branding Your Business

Everyone has a brand; either you create it, or it is created for you. Control your brand by creating a *Five-Point Branding Message*. The branding message is used to describe how you uniquely serve your clients. You and your team must be able to articulate the type of commitment you deliver and the value you add to the clients you serve. The *Five-Point Branding Message* is a way to successfully position you and your team as different from the alternatives the client has to select from. There are five main points to cover:

1. What you do to uniquely serve your clients?
2. How are you able to provide this level of service?
3. What are the vast resources you have available that support you providing this level of service?
4. How do you deliver this service in a highly personalized way?
5. Why you (your team)?

The Five-Point Branding Message can be used for several purposes, including:

- Creating interest in clients or prospects to meet with you,

- Creating interest in internal *or* external centers of influence to meet/introduce you,
- Establishing a vision for how you work with clients and the value you add, and
- Setting the framework with clients or prospects for examining their current situation so you can serve as a resource.

A brand is often perceived as a name, symbol, logo, or design that identifies and differentiates a product or service. But in reality, it's so much more than that. A brand is a representation of an emotional relationship between customers and the business. A brand is a person's instinctive feeling about a company. You can build your branding message as points. Each point is designed to generate interest and solicit more inquiry or interaction on behalf of your audience. Breaking your message into points allows you to use all or parts of the message, depending on the circumstances and situation. Your final branding message will be made up of phases and terms that are part of the strategy that differentiates you from the competition. Here's an example you can tweak from a commercial/residential sanitizing and cleaning service company:

Point 1—What you do to uniquely serve your clients?

"I work systematically with my clients to help keep their homes and businesses safe and healthy."

It is important to explain that you help manage all their sanitizing, disinfecting, and cleaning needs no matter what is on the top of their mind at the moment. Do not be limited by cleaning or disinfecting the property issues. Stress how all the these issues the client faces affect the overall sanitization of a healthy property that addresses the technology to kill germs, bacteria, allergens, mold, odors and viruses—including COVID-19. When you do this, clients or prospects are engaged by the fact that you are able to know that they may have an issue that is a priority or that you might be able to treat something that they may have overlooked. You are positioning what you do as a professional.

Point 2—How you are able to provide this level of service.

"Our trained professionals use state-of-the-art technology here at T&T Sanitizing and Cleaning Services that focuses on keeping homes and workplaces clean and productive. We support this approach by primarily helping to eliminate and avoid the spread of virus contamination (including coronavirus). We have found the use of bio-misting and bio-fogging, dispensed by an atomized sprayer, to be most appropriate for our clients. Our methodical process allows our team to prioritize your issues. As your situation reoccurs, we are there to provide repeat treatment applications."

Point 3—The vast resources you have available that support you in providing this level of service.

"I am supported by the vast resources of T&T Sanitizing and Cleaning Services that allow me to provide this high level of service. Let me take a few minutes to describe our team here at T&T Sanitizing and Cleaning Services:"

- Local family owned and operated business.
- Over twenty-five years of experience in health-care facilities management.
- Sanitizing, disinfecting, and cleaning experience.
- Our board chairman is an owner in the business with a PhD in Health Services Management.

Point 4—How you deliver this service in a highly personalized way?

"I deliver this service here at T&T Sanitizing and Cleaning Services in a highly personalized way. My team members are passionately committed to the individual client all the time. Protection and wellness are the key concerns in our community today as we continue to navigate back to normalcy during these challenging times under the current state of this pandemic. We are here to 'help keep you safe and healthy.' Our mission is to help families and businesses with environmental remediation to eliminate and avoid the spread of germs, contamination, bacteria, and viruses (including coronavirus)."

Point 5—Why you? Why T&T Sanitizing and Cleaning Services?

"Additionally, let me tell you a few ways that I offer unique value to my clients:"

1. I have a clear methodology for helping clients.
2. We articulate our process upfront.
3. We are experienced, disciplined, and focused.
4. We use CDC Approved, hospital grade disinfectants.

In conclusion, the branding message for T&T Sanitizing and Cleaning Service (as a script to be taught and learned) sounds like this:

> I work systematically with my clients to help keep their homes and businesses safe and healthy. I help manage all of their sanitizing, disinfecting and cleaning needs to kill germs, bacteria, allergens, mold, odors, and viruses—including

COVID-19. Our trained professionals use state-of-the-art technology here at T&T Sanitizing and Cleaning Services that focus on keeping homes and workplaces clean and productive. We support this approach by primarily helping to eliminate and avoid the spread of virus contamination (including coronavirus). We have found the use of Bio-misting and Bio-fogging, dispensed by an atomized sprayer to be most appropriate for our clients. Our methodical process allows our team to prioritize client issues. As your situation reoccurs, we are here to provide repeat treatment applications. "I am supported by the vast resources of T&T Sanitizing and Cleaning Services that allow us to provide this high level of service. Let me take a few minutes to describe our Team here at T&T Sanitizing and Cleaning Services.

- Local family owned and operated business.
- Over twenty-five years of experience health care facilities management.
- Sanitizing, disinfecting, and cleaning experience.
- Our board chairman is an owner in the business with a PhD in Health Services Management.

I deliver this service here at T&T Sanitizing and Cleaning Services in a highly personalized way. My team members are passionately committed to the individual client all of the time. Protection and wellness are the key concerns in our community today as we continue to navigate back to normalcy during these challenging times under the current state of this Pandemic. We are here to 'help keep you safe and healthy.' Our mission is to help families and businesses with environmental remediation to eliminate and avoid the spread of germs, contamination, bacteria, and viruses (including coronavirus). Additionally, let me tell you a few ways that I offer unique value to my clients:

- I have a clear methodology for helping clients.
- We articulate our process upfront.
- We are experienced, disciplined and focused.
- We use hospital grade disinfectants.

It's advisable to learn and remember all the features of your branding message. This will help you charm and educate your prospects using your *five points*. Many business owners have found success using different versions of their branding message, a short version and a shorter version. These versions are often referred to as an elevator speech. "An elevator speech is a clear, brief message or 'commercial' about you. It communicates who you are, what you're looking for, and how you can benefit an individual, a company or an organization. It's typically about thirty seconds, the time it takes people to ride from the top to the bottom of a building in an elevator." An elevator pitch is important because it communicates the most important aspects your business and services within that short amount of time. Here are a few examples:

Short Version

I work systematically with my clients to help keep their homes and businesses safe and healthy. We support this approach by primarily helping to eliminate and avoid the spread of virus contamination (including coronavirus). As a locally owned family business with over twenty-five years of health care facilities management experience, sanitizing, disinfecting, and cleaning has become our expertise. We deliver this service here at T&T Sanitizing and Cleaning in a highly personalized way. Protection and wellness are the key concerns in our community today as we continue to navigate back to normalcy during these challenging times under the current state of this pandemic.

Shorter Version

I represent a professional commercial and residential disinfecting, sanitizing, and cleaning service. With over twenty-five years of experience, our trained professionals use state-of-the-art technology to kill, germs, bacteria, allergens, and viruses (including the coronavirus). We help keep workplaces clean, safe, and productive.

Your branding message is your value proposition that will inspire, persuade, and motivate buyers to ultimately want your product or service. Practice, practice, practice your branding message. For whatever version you use, make sure you understand the key points surrounding each sentence. Most of all, never lose sight of your brand. Customers and prospects will always remember your brand. I've found that prospects are persuaded by discounts, inspired by good service, but motivated to purchase if they know and trust your brand.

CHAPTER 9

Growing Your Business

Before I address "growing your business," let's examine the difficulties a business owner may experience that may hinder business growth. According to a recent FRACTV study, here are a few top reasons why start-ups fail or do not experience growth:

1. No market need—business model not viable
2. Run out of cash
3. Not the right team
4. Get outcompeted
5. Pricing
6. Cost issues
7. Poor product
8. Lack business model
9. Poor marketing
10. Ignore customers
11. Lose focus
12. No financing
13. Legal challenges
14. Burnout
15. Failure to pivot

Too many business owners don't build a business; they build a job for themselves. These business owners end up imprisoned inside the very business they work so hard to build. If they don't show up each day or something happens to them, their business dies. No one wants to build a business, and then don't like it. That's crazy, right? A business may look good on the outside and great on the inside, but the business owner may still feel sort of trapped or discontented. Some of the reasons a business owner may feel trapped include the following:

- They're withdrawn.
- They don't have a support system.
- They're restless.
- They're depressed.
- They have low self-esteem.
- They have commitment issues.

These are just a few, but there are some remedies to help business owners that are trapped and want to take their life back. One of the most stressful ways to live your life is to live above your means. Many business owners tend to spend more than they earn and get stressed on a daily basis about their financial situation. *Live a lifestyle you can afford.* Your outlook determines the way you see your business, your customers, and your growth. Your mind has the power to make you see things negatively, or it has the power to inject positivity into every day. So start to think more positive thoughts, and you will notice both your mindset and your business changing and improving. *Realize that the business responds to you.* You know your business better than anyone else, so you know what direction your business should be following. Listen to your heart, and pursue the excellence that make your soul sing. *Follow your passion.* A big part of having self-respect and the respect of others in your business is being able to say no. It is important you are not being a pushover. Say yes to others only when you genuinely mean it, but don't put your business on hold. *Be honest and learn to say no.* And a few other strategies to help business owners who feel they're trapped are as follows:

- Be aware of your power and take responsibility.
- Start to live a healthy life.
- Do what makes you happy.

Business growth is the cornerstone of success and sustainability for every business owner. The formula to achieve such success may vary from business to business and industry to industry. However, I've found that this blueprint for growing a business will be of most help for most business owners.

Whether you're a for profit business, non-profit business, club, social/civic organization, fraternity, sorority, VFW American Legion, or the like… you will be able to apply the principles of the "growing your business" blueprint to continuously improve, reinvent and move towards more success and growth in you business or organization.

Summarizing this chapter. Growing your business is best understood as:

Get engaged.
Recognize opportunities through discovery.
Offer alternatives with flawless implementation.
Win through relationship management.

(*See* Exhibit 5—located at the end of this book: "Blueprint to Grow Your Business".)

CHAPTER 10

Communication Skills

All business owners need to master communication skills whether it be verbal or nonverbal. Mastering these skills and understanding the written and unwritten protocols will speak volumes for your ability to earn trust and loyalty with your prospects and customers. The verbal element of communication is all about the words that you choose and how they are heard and interpreted. It is important to remember that effective verbal communication cannot be fully isolated from nonverbal communication—your body language, tone of voice, and facial expressions, for example. Clarity of speech, remaining calm, and focused, being polite, and following some basic rules of etiquette will all aid the process of verbal communication.

According to a study done by the University of Connecticut, first impressions turn out to be sixty-seven percent accurate. So you must be able to develop a first impression that lasts! Our primary objective in meeting others is to create comfort, trust, and rapport—even with outside interruptions. The best way to establish credibility is appearance, verbal/nonverbal communication skills, and the value of the product/service—in that order!

There are a few obstacles to master in making first impressions:

- Brief acknowledgment—then ignored (change locations quickly)
- Physical contacts—be very careful
- "The detail check"—mandatory
- "Lombardi Time"—always be on time
- Eye contact and handshakes
- Introductions

In the event you want to accelerate closing that deal, you must understand the principles of the "One-Minute Close." Always arrive, early and use positive body language. Eye contact, friendliness, and posture is equally important. You must be well prepared and always have a meeting agenda. Creating comfort also gives you an edge. Proximity creates comfort. For example

- Use "The Power Perch"
- Armchair vs. sofa
- Remove the big desk
- Accept a beverage
- Exchange business cards
- Smile! And imitate behavior
- Sell yourself first!

Mastering the power of self-promotion gives you a unique advantage. People do business with those they trust. Keeping appointments, agreements, and commitments goes a long way in earning trust and loyalty. Articulating your big picture story often is an absolute requirement. Last but not the least, you should be compelled to keep in constant contact and be accessible.

One of my colleagues shared that "7% of the message is the words we use, 38% is through tone and voice inflection, and 55% is from nonverbal communication." Facial gestures and posture go hand-in-hand and can easily be interrupted. I encourage you to evaluate your performance in four areas: (1) your physical presence, (2) your posture, (3) your handshakes, and (4) your eye contact. Let's take a look at the elements that make up these components:

Physical Presence

- Energy and confidence with class
- Be contagious
- Presume, but never assume
- Phone presence

Posture

- Good posture = strong presence and better health
- Standing or sitting
- Look as if you belong

Handshake

- Slow the "American" fast pace
- Often the only physical contact in a business relationship
- Begin with eye contact—friendly and direct
- Be the one initiating the handshake
- Web-to-web/palm-to-palm
- Apply the same pressure
- Treat men and women equally
- Continue the handshake until you know the other's eye color

Eye Contact

- To gain trust and establish rapport
- Show confidence and respect
- Be mindful of cultural traditions

Have you ever heard of the "eighty percent rule?" I'm told that eighty percent of business decisions made each day are judgment calls. I believe that good verbal and nonverbal skills have something to do with this rule. The unwritten protocol of space probably has bearing on this rule as well. For example, when it comes to space, the safe zone is three to six feet, and invading personal space always present a violation.

A professional who wants to be perceived as having power or presence seldom wastes time overexplaining, apologizing, or justifying opinions. They do business in person whenever possible, use the power of silence, and they "match and mirror." Matching and mirroring build rapport quickly. Have you ever tried to "ape" others' actions? This along with being aware of your body language, energy level, facial expressions, tone of voice, vocabulary, and pace often builds credibility, especially when you are subtle with intelligence and mirror and match.

There are warning signs you should recognize that will alert you when your messages are not positively being received. These signs are called "deceptions." Here are a few tips for spotting deceptions:

- Incongruency between what is said and how it is said
- Person fails to maintain strong eye contact
- The same information is repeated several times
- Voice is high-pitched and louder than normal
- Eye shift—normally to the left
- Pupils become smaller

- Person swallows harder and more obviously
- Face is flushed and perspiring
- Person speaks faster
- Hand is placed in front of mouth when talking

Working your business practice, mastering communication skills, and attracting new customers will help you grow your business. You will also need to change to adapt to new circumstances. Evaluate how your operations compare with most effective and profitable enterprises, then use their most successful elements—the "best practices" in your own business. Using these business tools can help you manage and grow your business practice:

- Benchmarking
- Forecasting
- Financial planning
- Strategic planning
- Performance monitoring
- Technologies

Successfully running and growing a small business requires a great deal of time, energy, money, and other resources. If you want to increase your chances for success, focus on being as efficient as possible. You can improve productivity by delegating, remaining focused, utilizing tools, automating processes, and welcoming change. The steps you need to take to "grow your business" has already been written. Use your business plan as a guide. This will help you keep focused.

CHAPTER 11

Taxes and Write-Offs

Just like an individual, businesses must pay several different kinds of taxes, some easier to understand than others. Taxes for businesses come in several varieties: federal, state, and local. There are also different types of taxes depending on various business activities like selling taxable products or services, using equipment, owning business property, being self-employed versus having employees, and of course, making a profit.

If you are just starting your business, you need to know what taxes you'll be expected to pay. If your business has changed—if you have bought property or started hiring employees, for example—you'll need to know about the taxes associated with these activities.

Income Taxes

All businesses must pay tax on their income; that is, the business must pay tax on the profit of the company (the income of the business less deductible expenses). How that tax is paid depends on the form of the business.

Small businesses (sole proprietors and single-member LLCs), partners in partnerships, and S-corporation owners pay taxes through their personal income tax returns. The concept called pass-through tax is the same for all these business types.

Sole proprietors and single-member LLC members pay taxes by filing a Schedule C included with their personal return.

Partners in partnerships and multiple-member LLC owners file a partnership business tax return for information purposes only. The individual partners or LLC members pay income taxes from their share of the income of the business, by including this income in their personal returns.

Sales Tax on Products and Services Sold in Certain States

Businesses don't directly pay sales tax on products and services they sell. But if your business operates in a state that has state income tax, you must set up a system to collect, report, and pay state sales tax.

Merchants in most states are required to collect sales tax and pay it to the state department of revenue. Specific products and services are sales tax eligible, depending on state laws. Money must be collected from customers, reported, and paid on a regular basis.

Don't forget sales taxes for items you sell online, which many states now are requiring for specific types of sellers.

Property Tax on Business Property

If your business owns real property (real estate) like a building, your business must pay property tax to the local taxing authority, which is usually the city or county where the property is located.

The tax is based on assessed value, same as for personal property like a house. There are special considerations for paying property taxes when you sell a piece of business property (capital gains taxes may have to be paid, and you should consult with a tax professional for such matters).

Excise Taxes on Use and Consumption

Excise taxes are paid by a business for certain types of use or consumption like fuels and other activities like transportation and communication. Excise taxes are paid to the IRS, either quarterly or annually, depending upon usage, using Form 720.

Self-Employment Tax on Owner's Share of Business Income

Self-employment taxes are those paid by sole proprietors and partners for Social Security and Medicare based on the income of the business. Because business owners are not employees, there is no pay to withhold these taxes from, so self-employment tax is the alternative.

LLC owners also must also pay self-employment tax. Owners of corporations who work as employees do not have to pay self-employment tax.

Estimated Taxes for Business Owners

Because you are the owner of a business, income taxes and self-employment taxes are not withheld from business income. Therefore. you must figure out the amount of taxes you need to pay and keep track during the year.

You may also need to pay quarterly estimated taxes to avoid penalty and interest charges at tax time because IRS requires that these taxes be paid throughout the year.

Employment or Payroll Taxes Paid on Employee Earnings

Like sales taxes, some employment taxes are collected, reported, and paid. In this case, the taxes are paid to the IRS and the Social

Security Administration. Employment taxes are those paid by the owner of a business for several types of taxes based on the gross pay of employees. These include FICA taxes (for Social Security and Medicare), federal and state unemployment, and federal and state workers compensation taxes. Some of these taxes (unemployment tax, for example) aren't collected from employees, and they must be paid completely by the employer.

Gross Receipts Tax on Businesses in Some States

Most states have a state income tax for businesses. But some states, like Nevada and Texas, impose a gross receipts tax on businesses instead of a state income tax. In these states, gross receipts (revenues) of the business are taxed. Some states allow deductions for this tax, and some types of businesses are exempt in some states. Sole proprietorships are usually exempt from paying gross receipts taxes, but not from state income tax. Corporations and LLCs are most likely to pay gross receipts taxes determined by the fiduciary laws of the state in which they are located.

Franchise Taxes: Similar to Gross Receipts Tax

Some states charge franchise taxes to corporations based on the value of the company. These taxes are similar to a state income tax or a gross receipts tax. Sole proprietorships are not typically subjected to a franchise tax.

Dividend Tax on Corporate Shareholders

If you are an owner of a corporation, you are a shareholder. That means you pay income taxes on income you receive from dividends.

In respect to tax deductible expenses or write-offs, a business can generally deduct start-up and organizational expenses incurred during a company's first year of operation.

Top Tax Deductions for Small Business

- Car and truck expenses (most small businesses use a vehicle, such as a car, light truck, or van)
- Salaries and wages
- Contract labor
- Supplies
- Depreciation
- Rent on business property
- Utilities
- Taxes
- Insurance
- Repairs
- Commissions and fees
- Travel
- Entertainment
- Advertising/marketing…and much more
- Equipment and large purchases
- Office space

There is an extremely helpful IRS tax provision that gives a huge write-off advantage to small business. This is called Section 179. Some people think Section 179 of the IRS Tax Code is mysterious or complicated; it really isn't. Section 179 allows taxpayers to deduct the cost of certain property as an expense when the property is placed in service. The Section 179 deduction applies to tangible personal property such as machinery, equipment, software, and vehicles purchased for use in a trade or business.

Section 179 of the IRS Tax Code allows businesses to deduct the full purchase price of qualifying machinery, equipment, software and vehicles purchased or financed during the tax year. That means that if you buy (or lease) a piece of qualifying equipment, you can deduct the *full* purchase price from your gross income. It's an incentive created by the US government to encourage business owners to make capital investments in their business.

Why Use Section 179?

Successful businesses take advantage of legal tax incentives to help lower their operating costs. The Section 179 deduction is a tax incentive that is easy to use and gives businesses an incentive to invest in the business by adding capital equipment—equipment that they use to improve their operations and further increase revenue. In short, taking advantage of the Section 179 deduction will help your business add capital assets, while allowing you to keep more of your tax dollars.

As stated in H.R.1 a.k.a. The Tax Cuts and Jobs Act, the deduction limit for Section 179 is $1,000,000 for 2019 and beyond, while the limit on equipment purchases remains at a little over $2.5 million. There is also a hundred percent bonus depreciation deduction available for both new and used equipment after reaching the spending cap. Of course, you will consult your income tax professional regarding how these specifically apply to your business.

Advantages of Leasing and Financing

The obvious advantage to leasing or financing equipment and software, and then taking the Section 179 deduction is the fact that you can deduct the full amount of the equipment and software in the year of purchase even if you didn't pay the full amount of the purchase price during the year (for example: the asset was leased or financed). The amount you save in taxes can actually exceed the payments, making this a very bottom-line friendly deduction (you are reading this correctly; in many cases, the tax savings from the deduction will make your bank account larger than if you never financed the equipment in the first place).

What's the Difference between Section 179 and Bonus Depreciation?

Bonus depreciation is offered some years, and some years it isn't. Right now, it's being offered at one hundred percent. The most important difference is both new and used equipment qualify for the Section 179 deduction (as long as the used equipment is "new to you"), while bonus depreciation has only covered new equipment only until the most recent tax law passed. In a switch from recent years, the bonus depreciation now includes used equipment.

Bonus depreciation is useful to very large businesses spending more than the Section 179 spending capital (currently $2,500,000) on new capital equipment. Also, businesses with a net loss are still qualified to deduct some of the cost of new equipment and carry forward the loss. When applying these provisions, Section 179 is generally taken first, followed by bonus depreciation—unless the business had no taxable profit, because the unprofitable business is allowed to carry the loss forward to future years.

Material Goods that Generally Qualify for the Section 179 Deduction

Please keep in mind that to qualify for the Section 179 deduction, the equipment listed below must be purchased and put into use between January 1 and December 31 of the tax year you are claiming:

- Equipment (machines, etc.) purchased for business use
- Tangible personal property used in business
- Business vehicles with a gross vehicle weight in excess of 6,000 lbs. (*See* Section 179 vehicle deductions)
- Computers
- Computer "off-the-shelf" software
- Office furniture
- Office equipment
- Property attached to your building that is not a structural component of the building (i.e., a printing press, large manufacturing tools, and equipment)
- Partial business use (equipment that is purchased for business use and personal use—generally, your deduction will be based on the percentage of time you use the equipment for business purposes)
- Certain improvements to existing non-residential buildings: fire suppression, alarms and security systems, HVAC, and roofing

In summary, Section 179 really does help small businesses. By allowing businesses to deduct the full amount of the purchase price of equipment (up to certain limits), Section 179 is an awesome incentive for businesses to purchase, finance, or lease equipment and get a tax write-off. Companies taking advantage of Section 179 deductions aren't actually paying less taxes, they're just saving money in the year they made the purchase instead of over five or more years. This encourages small businesses to purchase more while not taking away from the overall tax revenue.

Business Personal Property Taxes

A business personal property tax is a levy imposed on business-owned property. The tax is levied by the jurisdiction where the property is located, and it includes tangible property that is not real property. Tangible property includes movable man-made objects that have a physical form and can be seen and touched.

Personal property taxes, also known as property taxes, are a form of taxation on what is termed personal property. In a business, all movable assets are termed personal property and are taxed annually. Additionally, some states tax personal property such as motor vehicles, boats, and aircraft.

In many states, there is a tax on business-owned personal property, which is imposed and collected by the local governments. Responsibility for the assessment of all personal property throughout these states usually rests with the Department of Assessments and Taxation.

Personal property generally includes furniture, fixtures, office and industrial equipment, machinery, tools, supplies, inventory, and any other property not classified as real property.

Failure to pay...the Comptroller's office can:

- file a lien against the corporation/LLC,
- file a lien against officers of the corporation/LLC,
- attach corporate/LLC assets,
- attach personal assets,
- dissolve the corporation/LLC, and
- issue a summons.

CHAPTER 12

Self-Evaluation Tool

In an effort to get the most out of your business, you must have a clear set of goals, as well as a set of steps to achieve those goals. It is not uncommon for business owners to overlook the importance of self-evaluation. Like evaluating the strengths and weaknesses of an employee, business owners can learn more about their performance after a self-assessment.

An assessment helps you determine how you're perceived by others. The lessons learned from an assessment will help you reflect on your accomplishments, identify your shortcomings, and enable you to set new goals for the future. You'll be able to define a path for your professional development. Thinking over the questions presented in the evaluation tool and considering your answers, you'll be able to realize what things you need to do to improve personal performance as a business owner and possibly impact your business growth and success.

As you evaluate yourself personally and also as the business owner, there will be many determinates that will come across your mind. Some business owners ponder the question, "Who is really in charge?" Being the owner does not always mean you are in charge. Some business owners are "hands-on" with a solid understanding of every aspect of their business. Other business owners prefer to delegate responsibilities and management duties while supervising from above. Regardless of your style, your business can be successful if you follow one simple rule: "In business and in life—you get what you inspect, not always what you expect."

You must keep your finger on the pulse of your business and the people you employ. Don't let yourself get comfortable and rest on your laurels. You cannot move forward by standing still. You must keep pace with the speed that is necessary to keep a business charging into a profitable and sustainable future. Do you truly have a grasp on what's happening in your business? Do you know enough about the day-to-day operations? Do you really know your employees and customers? What information are you looking at regularly that helps keep your finger on the pulse of your business?

Having key performance indicators in your business will give you greater clarity and confidence to know what actions to take to navigate your success. It is important to work smarter and learn to speak your results. People often say, "The results speak for themselves." Nope, this isn't true. You must give your results a voice. Some business owners use realistic and measurable criteria to measure value and validate how effectively a business is achieving its key business goals. Other than the use of performance indicators, I have found that "high touch" measures with employees and customers speak volumes for improving business success. For instance, listening, collaborating, being visible, being accessible, and just managing by wandering around yields trust and respect.

Demonstrating the willingness and ability to lead by example is key. That's how, trust, respect, and loyalty are earned. Take the drill sergeant who asks the new recruit to give him fifty push-ups, and the sergeant gets down with the recruit accomplishing his fifty while the recruit has only completed twenty-five. If you are not sure how the job is done or willing to do it yourself, when push comes to shove, do not be surprised when your staff reacts the same way.

Perhaps you are happy with your business and the ways you have made the business even stronger. I imagine you are an innovative and proactive, results-oriented leader and realize that the only constant in business is "change." If you weren't the boss, how would your employees or customers rate you? Business owner self-evaluation is vital part of dealing with "change." (*See* Exhibit 6 and Exhibit 7—located at the end of this book: "Self-Assessment for Business Owners"—"Business Owner Self-Assessment Test".)

CHAPTER 13

Secrets of Success

In this chapter, I will share with you some blueprints, secrets, and tips from my experiences to help you start, grow, and reengineer a successful business. There is really no secret to running a successful business. First, you have to know the rules. Then learn "best practices," and get help from the experts. The best blueprint to follow is: "There is no one way; there is only your way." There is an infinite number of paths to success; you have to choose your own road. The road may be long and winding, frequently bumpy, and sometimes under construction. As the pioneer of your journey, just focus on your passion, and the light at the end of the tunnel will guide your actions.

Becoming a successful entrepreneur can be a long journey. Some take the road less traveled, while others focus intensely on an opportunity where others see nothing. Success is not all about innovative thinking and breakthrough ideas. I've found that entrepreneurial success usually come from great executions, simply by being passionately driven to do whatever it takes and "to go all out." My dad once told me, "Find something that keeps you up late at night, something that is on your mind first thing in the morning and most of the day, and use that as your passion to make money."

Another tip that you've probably heard, "Your network is your net worth." Networking is not something you do when you have extra time. Abraham Lincoln said, "The best way to predict the future is to create it." Accordingly, the potential for business success surrounds your daily life. Using the power of networking can create your future to achieve success. I've learned to always be prepared to recognize opportunities in disguise. Tip: always carry your business cards and remember your "elevator" speech. When you are within three feet of a person, that person should know who you are and what you do.

Another blueprint for success is being familiar with certain terms related to the documents essential to managing business success. You should learn these terms and have a general understanding of what they mean and how they apply to your business. Here are examples of just a few:

- Contracts
- Operating Agreements
- Buy-Sell Agreement
- Board Resolution
- Liability Insurance
- Umbrella Insurance Policy
- Workmen's Comp. Insurance
- W-2
- Form 1099
- Independent Contractor Agreement
- Invoice
- Work Order
- Quotes/Estimates
- Revenues
- Gross Profit
- Cost of Goods sold

- Inventory
- Expenses
- Net Income
- Net Loss
- Depreciation
- Profit of Insurance Certificate
- Certificate of Good Standing
- Form W9
- Form W4
- Personal Property Taxes
- Purchases
- Business Mileage Rate
- Exit Strategy
- Lease vs. Buy Strategy
- Brake-Even Point
- Outsourcing
- Noncompete Agreement
- Confidentially Agreement

These are just a few of the terms that may relate to your business. Every business owner will be presented with some or most of these terms at some time during their reign. Understanding the purpose, use, and need for these instruments and terms will certainly give you the power and control help to manage your success.

In order to be successful in business, you must possess certain principles. These principles or terms of endearment become a reflection of you and the company you run. (*See* Exhibit 8—located at the end of this book: "Terms of Endearment.")

DR. ROBERT GREGORY

"Like in medicine a prescription without a diagnosis is malpractice." Checking the vitals, assessing, diagnosing, planning, implementing, and evaluating become the measurement that sharpens performance, drives sustainable growth, and manages cost.
—Dr. Robert Gregory

FOR MORE INFORMATION ON:

- Business Owner Coaching/Consulting
- Seminars
- Lecture Series
- Motivational Speaking Programs
- Business Turnaround Services
- Financial Advisory / Tax Services
- Financial Planning Advisory Services

CONTACT: DR. ROBERT GREGORY

Website: www.drrobertgregory.com

(443) 588-5073

EXHIBIT 1

A GUIDE TO ADVANTAGES OF LLCS

ADVANTAGE	C CORP	S CORP	LLC	PARTNERSHIP	SOLE PROPRIETOR
Owners have limited liability for business debts and obligations	✓	✓	✓		
Created by a state-level registration that usually protects the company name	✓	✓	✓		
Business duration can be perpetual	✓	✓	✓		
May have an unlimited number of owners	✓		✓	✓	✓
Owners need not be U.S. citizens or residents	✓		✓		
May issue shares of stock to attract investors	✓	✓			
Owners can report business profits and loss on their personal return		✓	✓	✓	✓
Owners can split profit and loss with the business for a lower overall tax rate	✓				
Permitted to distribute special allocations, under certain guidelines			✓	✓	
Not required to hold annual meetings or record meeting minutes			✓	✓	✓

EXHIBIT 2

BUSINESS START-UP CHECKLIST

- Choose the company name.
- Choose a resident agent.
- Obtain the tax ID #—FEIN.
- File the articles of organization.
- Create an operating agreement.
- Open a business bank account.
- Get a business credit/debit card.
- Set up accounting.
    The filing fee is approximately $100 (in most states).
    Processing time is about eight weeks.
    An additional $50 fee expedites processing (to one to two days—or same day).

Other Considerations (that may be applicable):

A. Depending on the nature of the business, you may be required to obtain a business license in the state in which you plan to do business.
B. Trader's license
C. Sales tax account and reporting
D. Unemployment account for employees
E. Personal property tax account and annual and reporting
F. Vendor's license

EXHIBIT 3

BUSINESS PLAN TEMPLATE

The business plan consists of a narrative and several financial worksheets. The narrative template is the body of the business plan. It contains more than 150 questions divided into several sections. Work through the sections in any order that you like, except for the "Executive Summary," which should be done last. Skip any questions that do not apply to your type of business. When you are finished writing your first draft, you'll have a collection of small essays on the various topics of the business plan. Then you'll want to edit them into a smooth-flowing narrative.

The real value of creating a business plan is not in having the finished product in hand; rather, the value lies in the process of researching and thinking about your business in a systematic way. The act of planning helps you to think things through thoroughly. Study and research if you are not sure of the facts, and look at your ideas critically. It takes time now, but avoids costly, perhaps disastrous, mistakes later.

This business plan is a generic model suitable for all types of businesses. However, you should modify it to suit your particular circumstances. Before you begin, review the section titled "Refining the Plan" found at the end. It suggests emphasizing certain areas depending upon your type of business (manufacturing, retail, service, etc.). It also has tips for fine-tuning your plan to make an effective presentation to investors or bankers. If this is why you're creating your plan, pay particular attention to your writing style. You will be judged by the quality and appearance of your work as well as by your ideas.

It typically takes several weeks to complete a good plan. Most of that time is spent in research and rethinking your ideas and assumptions. But then, that's the value of the process. So make time to do the job properly. Those who do, never regret the effort. And finally, be sure to keep detailed notes on your sources of information and on the assumptions underlying your financial data.

If you need assistance with your business plan, contact:

Gregory Financial

Services

at:
Website: www.drrobertgregory.com

(443) 588-5073

BUSINESS PLAN OWNERS

Your business name
Address Line 1
Address Line 2
City, ST ZIP Code
Telephone
Fax
E-mail

CONTENTS

I. Executive Summary 93
II. General Company Description 94
III. Products and Services 96
IV. Marketing Plan 97
V. Operational Plan 106
VI. Management and Organization 111
VII. Personal Financial Statement 112
VIII. Start-up Expenses and Capitalization 113
IX. Financial Plan 114
X. Appendices 118
XI. Refining the Plan 119

EXECUTIVE SUMMARY

Write this section last. We suggest that you make it two pages or fewer. Include everything that you would cover in a five-minute interview.

Explain the fundamentals of the proposed business: What will your product be? Who will your customers be? Who are the owners? What do you think the future holds for your business and your industry?

Make it enthusiastic, professional, complete, and concise.

If applying for a loan, state clearly how much you want, precisely how you are going to use it, and how the money will make your business more profitable, thereby ensuring repayment.

GENERAL COMPANY DESCRIPTION

What business will you be in? What will you do?

Mission Statement: Many companies have a brief mission statement, usually in thirty words or fewer, explaining their reason for being and their guiding principles. If you want to draft a mission statement, this is a good place to put it in the plan, followed by company goals and objectives.

Goals are destinations—where you want your business to be. Objectives are progress markers along the way to goal achievement. For example, a goal might be to have a healthy, successful company that is a leader in customer service and that has a loyal customer following. Objectives might be annual sales targets and some specific measures of customer satisfaction.

Business philosophy: What is important to you in business?

To whom will you market your products? (State it briefly here—you will do a more thorough explanation in the "Marketing Plan" section.)

Describe your industry. Is it a growth industry? What changes do you foresee in the industry, short-term and long-term? How will your company be poised to take advantage of them?

Describe your most important company strengths and core competencies. What factors will make the company succeed? What do you think your major competitive strengths will be? What background experience, skills, and strengths do you personally bring to this new venture?

Legal form of ownership: sole proprietor, partnership, corporation, limited liability corporation (LLC)? Why have you selected this form?

PRODUCTS AND SERVICES

Describe in depth your products or services (technical specifications, drawings, photos, sales brochures, and other bulky items belong in "Appendices").

What factors will give you competitive advantages or disadvantages? Examples include level of quality or unique or proprietary features.

What are the pricing, fee, or leasing structures of your products or services?

MARKETING PLAN

Market Research—Why?

No matter how good your product and your service, the venture cannot succeed without effective marketing. And this begins with careful, systematic research. It is very dangerous to assume that you already know about your intended market. You need to do market research to make sure you're on track. Use the business planning process as your opportunity to uncover data and to question your marketing efforts. Your time will be well spent.

Market Research—How?

There are two kinds of market research: primary and secondary.
Secondary research means using published information such as industry profiles, trade journals, newspapers, magazines, census data, and demographic profiles. This type of information is available in public libraries, industry associations, chambers of commerce, from vendors who sell to your industry, and from government agencies.
Start with your local library. Most librarians are pleased to guide you through their business data collection. You will be amazed at what is there. There are more online sources than you could possibly use. Your chamber of commerce has good information on the local area. Trade associations and trade publications often have excellent industry-specific data.

Primary research means gathering your own data. For example, you could do your own traffic count at a proposed location, use the yellow pages to identify competitors, and do surveys or focus group interviews to learn about consumer preferences. Professional market research can be very costly, but there are many books that show small business owners how to do effective research themselves.

In your marketing plan, be as specific as possible; give statistics, numbers, and sources. The marketing plan will be the basis, later on, of the all-important sales projection.

Economics

Facts about your industry:

- What is the total size of your market?
- What percent share of the market will you have? (This is important only if you think you will be a major factor in the market.)
- Current demand in target market.
- Trends in target market—growth trends, trends in consumer preferences, and trends in product development.
- Growth potential and opportunity for a business of your size.
- What barriers to entry do you face in entering this market with your new company? Some typical barriers are
    - high capital costs,
    - high production costs,
    - high marketing costs,
    - consumer acceptance and brand recognition,
    - training and skills,
    - unique technology and patents,
    - unions,

- shipping costs, and
- tariff barriers and quotas.
- And of course, how will you overcome the barriers?
- How could the following affect your company?
    - Change in technology
    - Change in government regulations
    - Change in the economy
    - Change in your industry

Product

In the "Products and Services" section, you described your products and services as you see them. Now describe them from your customers' point of view.

Features and Benefits

List all your major products or services. For each product or service, describe the most important features: what is special about it? Describe the benefits. That is, what will the product do for the customer?

Note the difference between features and benefits, and think about them. For example, a house that gives shelter and lasts a long time is made with certain materials and to a certain design; those are its features. Its benefits include pride of ownership, financial security, providing for the family, and inclusion in a neighborhood. You build features into your product so that you can sell the benefits.

What after-sales services will you give? Some examples are delivery, warranty, service contracts, support, follow-up, and refund policy.

Customers

Identify your targeted customers, their characteristics, and their geographic locations, otherwise known as their demographics.

The description will be completely different depending on whether you plan to sell to other businesses or directly to consumers. If you sell a consumer product, but sell it through a channel of distributors, wholesalers, and retailers, you must carefully analyze both the end consumer and the middleman businesses to which you sell.

You may have more than one customer group. Identify the most important groups. Then, for each customer group, construct what is called a demographic profile:

- Age
- Gender
- Location
- Income level
- Social class and occupation
- Education
- Other (specific to your industry)

For business customers, the demographic factors might be

- industry (or portion of an industry),
- location,
- size of firm,
- quality, technology, and price preferences, and
- others (specific to your industry).

Competition

What products and companies will compete with you? List your major competitors: (names and addresses).

Will they compete with you across the board or just for certain products, certain customers or in certain locations?

Will you have important indirect competitors? (For example, video rental stores compete with theaters, although they are different types of businesses.)

How will your products or services compare with the competition?

Use the "Competitive Analysis" table below to compare your company with your two most important competitors. In the first column are key competitive factors. Since these vary from one industry to another, you may want to customize the list of factors.

In the column labeled "Me," state how you honestly think you will stack up in customers' minds, giving yourself a grade of: A to D. Then check whether you think this factor will be a strength or a weakness for you. Sometimes it is hard to analyze our own weaknesses. Try to be very honest here. Better yet, get some disinterested strangers to assess you. This can be a real eye-opener. And remember that you cannot be all things to all people. In fact, trying to be causes many business failures because efforts become scattered and diluted. You want an honest assessment of your firm's strong and weak points.

Now analyze each major competitor. In a few words, state how you think they compare.

In the final column, estimate the importance of each competitive factor to the customer. 1 = critical; 5 = not very important.

Table 1: Competitive Analysis

Factor	Me	Strength	Weakness	Competitor A	Competitor B	Importance to Customer
Products						
Price						
Quality						
Selection						
Service						
Reliability						
Stability						
Expertise						
Company Reputation						
Location						
Appearance						
Sales Method						
Credit Policies						
Advertising						
Image						

Now, write a short paragraph stating your competitive advantages and disadvantages.

Niche

Now that you have systematically analyzed your industry, your product, your customers, and the competition, you should have a clear picture of where your company fits into the world.

In one short paragraph, define your niche, your unique corner of the market.

Strategy

Now outline a marketing strategy that is consistent with your niche.

Promotion

How will you get the word out to customers?

Advertising: What media, why, and how often? Why this mix and not some other?

Have you identified low-cost methods to get the most out of your promotional budget?

Will you use methods other than paid advertising, such as trade shows, catalogs, dealer incentives, word of mouth (how will you stimulate it?), and network of friends or professionals?

What image do you want to project? How do you want customers to see you?

In addition to advertising, what plans do you have for graphic image support? This includes things like logo design, cards and letterhead, brochures, signage, and interior design (if customers come to your place of business).

Should you have a system to identify repeat customers and then systematically contact them?

Promotional Budget

How much will you spend on the items listed above?

Before start-up? (These numbers will go into your start-up budget.)

Ongoing? (These numbers will go into your operating plan budget.)

Pricing

Explain your method or methods of setting prices. For most small businesses, having the lowest price is not a good policy. It robs you of needed profit margin; customers may not care as much about price as you think; and large competitors can underprice you anyway. Usually, you will do better to have average prices and compete on quality and service.

Does your pricing strategy fit with what was revealed in your competitive analysis?

Compare your prices with those of the competition. Are they higher, lower, the same? Why?

How important is price as a competitive factor? Do your intended customers really make their purchase decisions mostly on price?

What will be your customer service and credit policies?

Proposed Location

You may not have a precise location picked out yet. This is the time to think about what you want and need in a location. Many start-ups run successfully from home for a while.

You will describe your physical needs later, in the "Operational Plan" section. Here, analyze your location criteria as they will affect your customers.

Is your location important to your customers? If yes, how?

If customers come to your place of business, is it convenient? Parking? Interior spaces? Not out of the way?

Is it consistent with your image?

Is it what customers want and expect?

Where is the competition located? Is it better for you to be near them (like car dealers or fast-food restaurants) or distant (like convenience food stores)?

Distribution Channels

How do you sell your products or services?

- Retail
- Direct (mail order, Web, catalog)
- Wholesale
- Your own sales force
- Agents
- Independent representatives
- Bid on contracts

Sales Forecast

Now that you have described your products, services, customers, markets, and marketing plans in detail, it's time to attach some numbers to your plan. Use a sales forecast spreadsheet to prepare a month-by-month projection. The forecast should be based on your historical sales, the marketing strategies that you have just described, your market research, and industry data, if available.

You may want to do two forecasts: (1) a "best guess," which is what you really expect and (2) a "worst case" low estimate that you are confident you can reach no matter what happens.

Remember to keep notes on your research and your assumptions as you build this sales forecast and all subsequent spreadsheets in the plan. This is critical if you are going to present it to funding sources.

OPERATIONAL PLAN

Explain the daily operation of the business, its location, equipment, people, processes, and surrounding environment.

Production

How and where are your products or services produced? Explain your methods of:

- production techniques and costs,
- quality control,
- customer service,
- inventory control, and
- product development.

Location

What qualities do you need in a location? Describe the type of location you'll have.

Physical requirements

- Amount of space
- Type of building
- Zoning
- Power and other utilities

Access

Is it important that your location be convenient to transportation or to suppliers?

Do you need easy walk-in access?

What are your requirements for parking and proximity to freeway, airports, railroads, and shipping centers?

Include a drawing or layout of your proposed facility if it is important, as it might be for a manufacturer.

Construction

Most new companies should not sink capital into construction, but if you are planning to build, costs and specifications will be a big part of your plan.

Cost

Estimate your occupation expenses, including rent, but also including maintenance, utilities, insurance, and initial remodeling costs to make the space suit your needs. These numbers will become part of your financial plan. What will be your business hours?

Legal Environment

Describe the following:

- Licensing and bonding requirements
- Permits
- Health, workplace, or environmental regulations
- Special regulations covering your industry or profession
- Zoning or building code requirements

- Insurance coverage
- Trademarks, copyrights, or patents (pending, existing, or purchased)

Personnel

- Number of employees.
- Type of labor (skilled, unskilled, and professional).
- Where and how will you find the right employees?
- Quality of existing staff.
- Pay structure.
- Training methods and requirements.
- Who does which tasks?
- Do you have schedules and written procedures prepared?
- Have you drafted job descriptions for employees? If not, take time to write some. They really help internal communications with employees.
- For certain functions, will you use contract workers in addition to employees?

Inventory

- What kind of inventory will you keep: raw materials, supplies, finished goods?
- Average value in stock (i.e., what is your inventory investment?)
- Rate of turnover and how this compares to the industry averages?
- Seasonal buildups?
- Lead time for ordering?

Suppliers

Identify key suppliers:

- Names and addresses
- Type and amount of inventory furnished
- Credit and delivery policies
- History and reliability

Should you have more than one supplier for critical items (as a backup)?

Do you expect shortages or short-term delivery problems?

Are supply costs steady or fluctuating? If fluctuating, how would you deal with changing costs?

Credit Policies

- Do you plan to sell on credit?
- Do you really need to sell on credit? Is it customary in your industry and expected by your clientele?
- If yes, what policies will you have about who gets credit and how much?
- How will you check the creditworthiness of new applicants?
- What terms will you offer your customers; that is, how much credit and when is payment due?
- Will you offer prompt payment discounts? (Hint: Do this only if it is usual and customary in your industry.)
- Do you know what it will cost you to extend credit? Have you built the costs into your prices?

Managing Your Accounts Receivable

If you do extend credit, you should do an aging, at least monthly, to track how much of your money is tied up in credit given to customers and to alert you to slow payment problems. A receivables aging looks like the following table:

	Total	Current	30 Days	60 Days	90 Days	Over 90 Days
Accounts Receivable Aging						

You will need a policy for dealing with slow-paying customers:

- When do you make a phone call?
- When do you send a letter?
- When do you get your attorney to threaten?

Managing Your Accounts Payable

You should also age your accounts payable, what you owe to your suppliers. This helps you plan whom to pay and when. Paying too early depletes your cash, but paying late can cost you valuable discounts and can damage your credit. (Hint: If you know you will be late making a payment, call the creditor before the due date.)

Do your proposed vendors offer prompt payment discounts?

A payables aging looks like the following table:

	Total	Current	30 Days	60 Days	90 Days	Over 90 Days
Accounts Payable Aging						

MANAGEMENT AND ORGANIZATION

Who will manage the business on a day-to-day basis? What experience does that person bring to the business? What special or distinctive competencies? Is there a plan for continuation of the business if this person is lost or incapacitated?

If you'll have more than ten employees, create an organizational chart showing the management hierarchy and who is responsible for key functions.

Include position descriptions for key employees. If you are seeking loans or investors, include résumés of owners and key employees.

Professional and Advisory Support

List the following:

- Board of directors
- Management advisory board
- Attorney
- Accountant
- Insurance agent
- Banker
- Consultant or consultants
- Mentors and key advisers

PERSONAL FINANCIAL STATEMENT

Include personal financial statements for each owner and major stockholder, showing assets and liabilities held outside the business and personal net worth. Owners will often have to draw on personal assets to finance the business, and these statements will show what is available. Bankers and investors usually want this information as well.

START-UP EXPENSES AND CAPITALIZATION

You will have many start-up expenses before you even begin operating your business. It's important to estimate these expenses accurately, and then to plan where you will get sufficient capital. This is a research project, and the more thorough your research efforts, the less chance that you will leave out important expenses or underestimate them.

Even with the best of research, however, opening a new business has a way of costing more than you anticipate. There are two ways to make allowances for surprise expenses. The first is to add a little "padding" to each item in the budget. The problem with that approach, however, is that it destroys the accuracy of your carefully wrought plan. The second approach is to add a separate line item, called contingencies, to account for the unforeseeable. This is the approach we recommend.

Talk to others who have started similar businesses to get a good idea of how much to allow for contingencies. If you cannot get good information, we recommend a rule of thumb that contingencies should equal at least 20 percent of the total of all other start-up expenses.

Explain your research and how you arrived at your forecasts of expenses. Give sources, amounts, and terms of proposed loans. Also explain in detail how much will be contributed by each investor and what percent ownership each will have.

FINANCIAL PLAN

The financial plan consists of a twelve-month profit and loss projection, a four-year profit and loss projection (optional), a cash flow projection, a projected balance sheet, and a break-even calculation. Together they constitute a reasonable estimate of your company's financial future. More important, the process of thinking through the financial plan will improve your insight into the inner financial workings of your company.

Twelve-Month Profit and Loss Projection

Many business owners think of the twelve-month profit and loss projection as the centerpiece of their plan. This is where you put it all together in numbers and get an idea of what it will take to make a profit and be successful.

Your sales projections will come from a sales forecast in which you forecast sales, cost of goods sold, expenses, and profit month-by-month for one year.

Profit projections should be accompanied by a narrative explaining the major assumptions used to estimate company income and expenses.

Research notes: Keep careful notes on your research and assumptions, so that you can explain them later if necessary, and also, so that you can go back to your sources when it's time to revise your plan.

Four-Year Profit Projection (Optional)

The twelve-month projection is the heart of your financial plan. The four-year profit projection is for those who want to carry their forecasts beyond the first year.

Of course, keep notes of your key assumptions, especially about things that you expect will change dramatically after the first year.

Projected Cash Flow

If the profit projection is the heart of your business plan, cash flow is the blood. Businesses fail because they cannot pay their bills. Every part of your business plan is important, but none of it means a thing if you run out of cash.

The point of this worksheet is to plan how much you need before start-up for preliminary expenses, operating expenses, and reserves. You should keep updating it and using it afterward. It will enable you to foresee shortages in time to do something about them—perhaps cut expenses or perhaps negotiate a loan. But foremost, you shouldn't be taken by surprise.

There is no great trick to preparing it: the cash-flow projection is just a forward look at your checking account.

For each item, determine when you actually expect to receive cash (for sales) or when you will actually have to write a check (for expense items).

You should track essential operating data, which is not necessarily part of cash flow but allows you to track items that have a heavy impact on cash flow, such as sales and inventory purchases.

You should also track cash outlays prior to opening in a pre-start-up column. You should have already researched those for your start-up expenses plan.

Your cash flow will show you whether your working capital is adequate. Clearly, if your projected cash balance ever goes negative, you will need more start-up capital. This plan will also predict just when and how much you will need to borrow.

Explain your major assumptions, especially those that make the cash flow differ from the profit and loss projection. For example, if you make a sale in month one, when do you actually collect the cash? When you buy inventory or materials, do you pay in advance, upon delivery, or much later? How will this affect cash flow?

Are some expenses payable in advance? When?

Are there irregular expenses, such as quarterly tax payments, maintenance and repairs, or seasonal inventory buildup that should be budgeted?

Loan payments, equipment purchases, and owner's draws usually do not show on profit and loss statements but definitely do take cash out. Be sure to include them.

And of course, depreciation does not appear in the cash flow at all because you never write a check for it.

Opening-Day Balance Sheet

A balance sheet is one of the fundamental financial reports that any business needs for reporting and financial management. A balance sheet shows what items of value are held by the company (assets) and what its debts are (liabilities). When liabilities are subtracted from assets, the remainder is owners' equity.

Use a start-up expenses and capitalization spreadsheet as a guide to preparing a balance sheet as of opening day. Then detail how you calculated the account balances on your opening day balance sheet.

Optional: Some people want to add a projected balance sheet showing the estimated financial position of the company at the end of the first year. This is especially useful when selling your proposal to investors.

Break-Even Analysis

Break-even sales is the dollar amount of revenue at which a business earns a profit of zero. This amount exactly covers the underlying fixed expenses of the business as well as the variable expenses associated with the sales.

(Where fixed costs are expressed in dollars, but variable costs are expressed as a percent of total sales.)

Include all assumptions upon which your break-even calculation is based.

APPENDICES

Include details and studies used in your business plan; for example,

- brochures and advertising materials,
- industry studies,
- blueprints and plans,
- maps and photos of location,
- magazine or other articles,
- detailed lists of equipment owned or to be purchased,
- copies of leases and contracts,
- letters of support from future customers,
- any other materials needed to support the assumptions in this plan,
- market research studies, and
- list of assets available as collateral for a loan.

REFINING THE PLAN

The generic business plan presented above should be modified to suit your specific type of business and the audience for which the plan is written.

For Raising Capital

For Bankers

- Bankers want assurance of orderly repayment. If you intend using this plan to present to lenders, include:
  - amount of loan; how the funds will be used;
  - what this will accomplish (how will it make the business stronger?);
  - requested repayment terms (number of years to repay)—you will probably not have much negotiating room on interest rate but may be able to negotiate a longer repayment term, which will help cash flow; and
  - collateral offered and a list of all existing liens against collateral.

For Investors

- Investors have a different perspective. They are looking for dramatic growth, and they expect to share in the rewards:
  o Funds needed short-term
  o Funds needed in two to five years
  o How the company will use the funds and what this will accomplish for growth
  o Estimated return on investment
  o Exit strategy for investors (buyback, sale, or IPO)
  o Percent of ownership that you will give up to investors
  o Milestones or conditions that you will accept
  o Financial reporting to be provided
  o Involvement of investors on the board or in management

For Type of Business

Manufacturing

- Planned production levels
- Anticipated levels of direct production costs and indirect (overhead) costs—how do these compare to industry averages (if available)?
- Prices per product line
- Gross profit margin, overall and for each product line
- Production/capacity limits of planned physical plant
- Production/capacity limits of equipment
- Purchasing and inventory management procedures
- New products under development or anticipated to come online after start-up

Service Businesses

- Service businesses sell intangible products. They are usually more flexible than other types of businesses, but they also have higher labor costs and generally very little in fixed assets.
- What are the key competitive factors in this industry?
- Your prices.
- Methods used to set prices.
- System of production management.
- Quality control procedures. Standard or accepted industry quality standards.
- How will you measure labor productivity?
- Percent of work subcontracted to other firms. Will you make a profit on subcontracting?
- Credit, payment, and collections policies and procedures.
- Strategy for keeping client base.

High-Technology Companies

- Economic outlook for the industry.
- Will the company have information systems in place to manage rapidly changing prices, costs, and markets?
- Will you be on the cutting edge with your products and services?
- What is the status of research and development? And what is required to bring product/service to market and keep the company competitive?
- How does the company protect intellectual property, avoid technological obsolescence, supply necessary capital, and retain key personnel?

High-tech companies sometimes have to operate for a long time without profits and sometimes even without sales. If this fits your situation, a banker probably will not want to lend to you. Venture capitalists may invest, but your story must be very good. You must do long-term financial forecasts to show when profit takeoff is expected to occur. And your assumptions must be well-documented and well-argued.

Retail Business

- Company image
- Pricing
    - Explain markup policies.
    - Prices should be profitable, competitive, and in accordance with company image.

- Inventory
    - Selection and price should be consistent with company image.
    - Inventory level: Find industry average numbers for annual inventory turnover rate (available in RMA book). Multiply your initial inventory investment by the average turnover rate. The result should be at least equal to your projected first year's cost of goods sold. If it is not, you may not have enough budgeted for start-up inventory.

- Customer service policies: These should be competitive and in accord with company image.
- Location: Does it give the exposure that you need? Is it convenient for customers? Is it consistent with company image?

- Promotion: Methods used, cost. Does it project a consistent company image?
- Credit: Do you extend credit to customers? If yes, do you really need to, and do you factor the cost into prices?

EXHIBIT 4

DR. GREGORY'S PRESCRIPTION FOR GETTING THINGS DONE

Step 1:   Set goals.
Step 2:   Determine how you are spending your time.
Step 3:   Develop a time management chart.
Step 4:   Create a "to do" list the right way.
Step 5:   Create a "not to do" list.
Step 6:   Give yourself an extra hour every day.
Step 7:   Spend time planning and organizing.
Step 8:   Do the right thing right.
Step 9:   Eliminate the urgent.
Step 10: Learn to say no.
Step 11: Learn to stay focused.
Step 12: Bundle tasks.
Step 13: Align your work style and work area.
Step 14: Beware of multitasking.
Step 15: Plan for tomorrow today.
Step 16: Organize your work area.
Step 17: Give yourself time to change gears.
Step 18: Conquer procrastination.
Step 19: Write things down.
Step 20: Review your accomplishments.
Step 21: Never stop improving your time management.

EXHIBIT 5

Blueprint to Grow Your Business

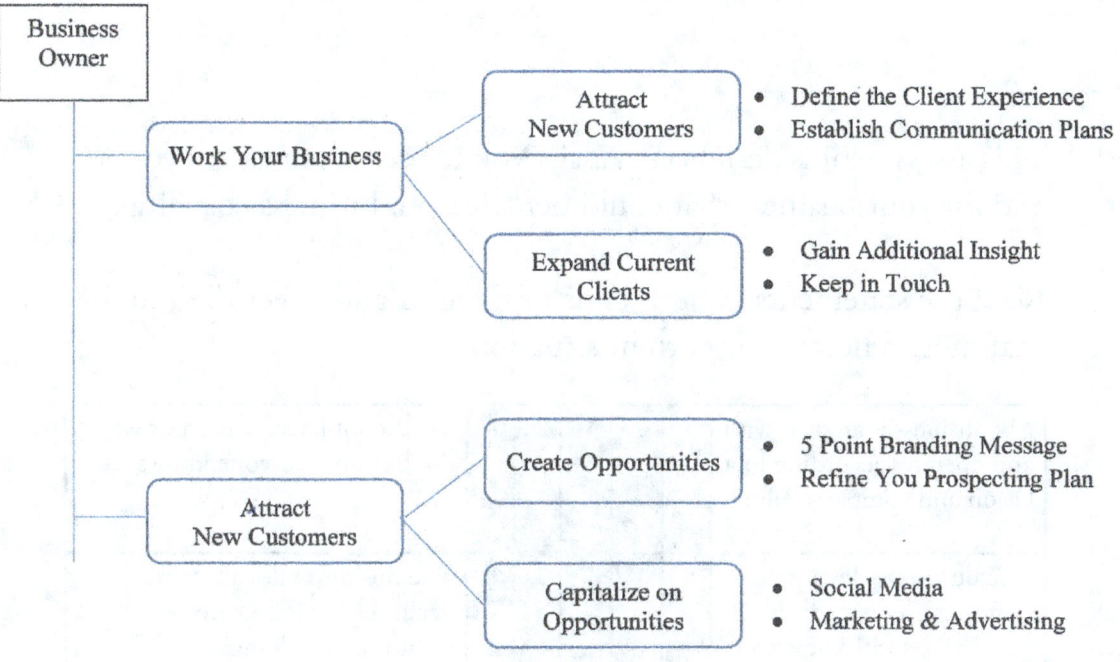

EXHIBIT 6

SELF-ASSESSMENT FOR BUSINESS OWNERS

This assessment is designed to assist you to identify areas for yourself and for your business that could benefit from business coaching.

Read the statements at both ends of the grid and select the number that most reflects your current situation.

My business is aligned with and operates according to a vision and company values.	5	4	3	2	1	We do not have a vision or we do, but not everyone knows it.
The business sales are trending up on a consistent basis, and I know this because I measure them.	5	4	3	2	1	The business sales are flat, declining, or I am sure what they are doing?
We know where our profits come from and how much each line item gives us.	5	4	3	2	1	I know we make money because we can pay our bills, but I am not sure what my margins are or where the profits come from.
We are consistently successful at reaching our goals.	5	4	3	2	1	We don't have goals, or we have a hard time reaching our goals.

GUIDE FOR BUSINESS START-UPS AND EXISTING BUSINESSES

Our business is thriving and so are our employees.	5	4	3	2	1	We are often short of necessities, such as time, space, opportunity, money, or resources.
I have an exit strategy.	5	4	3	2	1	When I go the, business goes too.
We have a written strategic plan and make conscientious decisions based on that plan.	5	4	3	2	1	We are "winging it."
We watch and understand cash flow.	5	4	3	2	1	We are constantly chasing receivables.
We leverage our strengths and move quickly on new opportunities.	5	4	3	2	1	We feel like we are a step behind and miss opportunities.
We attract business and business interest easily. We have the kind of customer/client we want.	5	4	3	2	1	We have customers/clients that we do not like, but we feel we have to keep them; they drain our time and resources.
I have a lot of support personally and professionally.	5	4	3	2	1	There is no one to talk to about the above.
I am well-organized and protected financially.	5	4	3	2	1	I am sinking in debt.

GFS — GREGORY FINANCIAL SERVICES

Robert Gregory, Ph.D., MBA, QPFC
(443) 506-7996
Website: www.drrobertgregory.com

EXHIBIT 7

BUSINESS OWNER SELF-ASSESSMENT TEST

Expert Growth-Focused Partner

Self-assessment test:
Are you ready to be a business owner?

Type of skill	Your Score	Bad to fair	Fair		Good
SALES					
Setting prices	1	2	3	4	5
Buying raw materials/stock	1	2	3	4	5
Sales planning	1	2	3	4	5
Negotiating	1	2	3	4	5
Direct selling to buyers	1	2	3	4	5
Customer service follow-up	1	2	3	4	5
Managing other sales reps	1	2	3	4	5
Tracking competitors	1	2	3	4	5
Average Score, divide by 8:					

Marketing

Advertising/promotion/PR	1	2	3	4	5
Developing marketing plans	1	2	3	4	5
Developing marketing strategies	1	2	3	4	5
Distribution planning	1	2	3	4	5

GUIDE FOR BUSINESS START-UPS AND EXISTING BUSINESSES

Packaging	1	2	3	4	5
Average Score, divide by 5:					

Financial Planning

Cash flow planning	1	2	3	4	5
Monthly financial management	1	2	3	4	5
Bank relationships	1	2	3	4	5
Management of credit lines	1	2	3	4	5
Average Score, divide by 4:					

Type of skill	Very bad	Bad to fair	Fair	Good	Excellent

Accounting

Bookkeeping	1	2	3	4	5
Billing, payables, receivables	1	2	3	4	5
Monthly profit and loss statements	1	2	3	4	5
Tax preparation	1	2	3	4	5
Average Score (Add circled numbers together, divide by 4):					

Administrative

Scheduling	1	2	3	4	5
Payroll handling	1	2	3	4	5
Benefits administration	1	2	3	4	5
Average Score (Add circled numbers together, divide by 3):					

Personnel Management

Hiring employees	1	2	3	4	5
Firing employees	1	2	3	4	5
Motivating employees	1	2	3	4	5
General management skills	1	2	3	4	5
Average Score (Add circled numbers together, divide by 4):					

Personal Business Skills

Oral presentation skills	1	2	3	4	5
Written communication skills	1	2	3	4	5
Computer skills	1	2	3	4	5
Word processing skills	1	2	3	4	5
Fax, e-mail experience	1	2	3	4	5
Organizational skills	1	2	3	4	5
Average Score (Add circled numbers together, divide by 6):					

Intangibles

Ability to work long and hard	1	2	3	4	5
Ability to manage risk and stress	1	2	3	4	5
Support from your family	1	2	3	4	5
Ability to deal with failure	1	2	3	4	5
Ability to work on your own	1	2	3	4	5
Ability to work with and manage others	1	2	3	4	5
Average Score (Add circled numbers together, divide by 6):					

The total of all your average scores:

Now find out what your score means

- *if your total is less than 20*

There are a lot of areas you still need to work on before you'll be ready to start your own business. Look at all the items in the tables above that you have scored 1 or 2, and spend the next few months learning as much as you can about these topics.

- *if your total is between 20 and 25*

You have the potential to be a successful business owner, but there are still quite a few areas that you need to get better at. If you start a business now, it could prove to be much tougher than you think.

- *if your total is above 25*

Well done! If your skills are as good as you think they are, you are ready to start a new business!

EXHIBIT 8

TERMS OF ENDEARMENT

1. Improve the lives of others.
2. Build value—deliver value.
3. Be authentic.
4. Be transparent (full disclosure).
5. Treat every customer like they are your only customer.
6. Heed the lessons of failure.
7. "Work like there is someone working twenty-four hours a day to take it all away from you."
8. Line up your customers before you open your doors.
9. Retain your customers.
10. Adapt to change.
11. Recharge your own batteries (take breaks, reexamine your goals, learn new skills).
12. Invest in yourself.
13. Eliminate all needless busy work.
14. Have a consistent morning routine.
15. Do what needs to be done—today.

ABOUT THE AUTHOR

Dr. Robert Gregory is a trusted business adviser, author, publisher (quarterly business owner newsletter), motivational speaker, business owner coach, tax advisor, estate planning adviser, and a successful entrepreneur. Before starting his companies, Dr. Gregory held senior executive positions in several industries: wealth management, banking, health care, and real estate.

Born in 1952, in Baltimore, Maryland, Dr. Gregory graduated with a Bachelor of Arts degree in accounting from Loyola University in 1974. He also earned his MBA and his PhD is from LaSalle University.

Dr. Gregory is a high-energy, fiscally conscious, goal-driven coach with a flair for innovation and creative problem-solving. He has a strong passion for business and thoroughly enjoys sharing his experiences, mentoring, motivating and inspiring others despite their circumstance.

He has also published numerous articles to inform and educate small business owners. He has been a columnist for several newspapers, and has made guest appearances on many radio broadcasts.

www.ingramcontent.com/pod-product-compliance
Lightning Source LLC
Chambersburg PA
CBHW081710220526

45466CB00009B/2949